FUEL YOUR FIRE

Fuel Your Fire
by Digvijay Mourya
Paperback Edition

First published in India in 2023 by

Inkfeathers Publishing
Vivek Vihar, New Delhi
www.inkfeathers.com

ISBN 978-81-19483-39-6

FUEL YOUR FIRE

The Explosive Power of Mindset with Purpose

DIGVIJAY MOURYA

Inkfeathers Publishing
www.inkfeathers.com

DEDICATION

This book is dedicated to all the leaders and sales professionals who have the courage and determination to pursue their dreams and achieve their goals. Your hard work, passion, and commitment to excellence is an inspiration to me.

I would also like to dedicate this book to my family, loved ones and my office colleagues, my Directors Mr. Deepak Verma & Mr. Praveen Verma, who have supported me throughout my journey. Your unwavering love, encouragement, and understanding have been instrumental in my success, and I am grateful for your constant support and belief in me.

Finally, I dedicate this book to all the readers, who have chosen to invest their time and energy in learning and growing. I hope that this book will provide you with the knowledge, skills, and inspiration you need to succeed in leadership and sales, and that it will help you achieve your own version of success.

Thank you for joining me on this journey, and I wish you all the best in your pursuit of excellence.

PREFACE

In a world where challenges and obstacles are a constant part of our journey, it is the power of mindset and purpose that can truly transform our lives. How we perceive and respond to the circumstances that surround us, and the clarity with which we define our purpose, can shape our actions, decisions, and ultimately, our destinies.

The power of mindset lies in our ability to cultivate a positive and resilient attitude towards life. It is the lens through which we view the world, and it determines whether we see opportunities or setbacks, possibilities or limitations. With a growth mindset, we embrace challenges as opportunities for growth, and failures as stepping stones towards success. We understand that our beliefs and thoughts have the power to influence our actions and shape our reality. By cultivating a mindset of optimism, perseverance, and self-belief, we can overcome adversity, learn from our experiences, and unlock our full potential.

Equally important is the power of purpose. A clear sense of purpose provides us with direction, meaning, and motivation. It is the driving force behind our actions and the source of our passion and perseverance. When we have a strong sense of purpose, we are able to navigate through life's ups and downs with resilience and determination. It fuels our commitment, ignites our creativity, and empowers us to make a positive difference in the world. Purpose gives our lives depth and fulfillment, as we align our actions and decisions with something greater than ourselves.

This book explores the profound impact that mindset and purpose can have on our personal and professional lives. It delves into the strategies and practices that enable us to cultivate a growth mindset, overcome limiting beliefs, and harness the power of positive thinking. It also explores the process of discovering and defining our purpose, and provides guidance on how to align our actions and goals with our deepest values and aspirations.

By embracing the power of mindset and purpose, we have the opportunity to shape our lives and contribute to a better world. Together, let us journey towards a future where positivity, purpose, and limitless potential reign supreme.

Part I

THE POWER OF MINDSET

Mindset refers to the set of beliefs, attitudes, and assumptions that we hold about ourselves, others, and the world around us. Our mindset shapes the way we perceive and respond to the events and challenges in our lives, and it can have a profound impact on our behaviors, emotions, and overall well-being.

A positive and growth-oriented mindset can lead to numerous benefits:

1. **Increased resilience:** People with a growth mindset are better able to bounce back from setbacks and challenges, as they view them as opportunities for learning and growth.
2. **Improved motivation:** Individuals with a growth mindset tend to be more motivated to learn, improve, and succeed, as they believe their efforts can lead to positive outcomes.
3. **Greater creativity and innovation:** A growth mindset encourages individuals to approach problems with an open and curious mindset, leading to more innovative and creative solutions.
4. **Better relationships:** People with a growth mindset tend to have stronger and more positive relationships, as they are more open to feedback, willing to learn from others, and able to empathize with different perspectives.

In contrast, a fixed mindset, which involves the belief that our abilities and traits are fixed and unchangeable, can lead to feelings of helplessness, limited learning, and decreased well-being.

Mindset affects performance: Research has shown that individuals with a growth mindset tend to perform better in academic, athletic, and professional settings. This is because they are more willing to take risks, persist in the face of challenges, and seek out feedback and learning opportunities.

Mindset affects health: Our mindset can also impact our physical health. Studies have found that individuals with a positive outlook and growth mindset tend to have lower levels of stress, better immune function, and a lower risk of chronic diseases like heart disease and diabetes.

Mindset affects happiness: Our mindset can also impact our overall sense of happiness and well-being. People with a growth mindset tend to be more optimistic, grateful, and satisfied with their lives, as they focus on learning, growth, and progress rather than fixed outcomes.

Mindset can be changed: The good news is that our mindset is not fixed and can be changed through intentional effort and practice. By cultivating a growth mindset, we can learn to embrace challenges, seek out feedback, and view failures as opportunities for learning and growth.

Mindset affects decision-making: Our mindset can also influence the decisions we make in our personal and professional lives. A growth mindset encourages us to consider multiple perspectives, challenge our assumptions, and make decisions based on what we can learn and grow from. In contrast, a fixed mindset may lead us to make decisions based on fear, insecurity, or a desire to avoid failure.

Mindset impacts leadership: Leaders with a growth mindset tend to be more effective in motivating and inspiring their teams, as they encourage their employees to take risks, learn from their mistakes, and embrace challenges. They also tend to be more open-minded, adaptive, and innovative in their approach to problem-solving.

Mindset is contagious: Our mindset can also impact those around us. When we adopt a growth mindset, we can inspire and encourage others to do the same. This can create a positive ripple effect within our social and professional networks, leading to greater collaboration, learning, and growth.

Mindset can help us achieve our goals: By adopting a growth mindset, we can set and achieve meaningful goals in our personal and professional lives. A growth mindset helps us stay focused on the process of learning and improvement, rather than the outcome, which can increase our motivation, persistence, and resilience in the face of challenges.

Mindset affects learning: Our mindset plays a crucial role in how we approach learning. A growth mindset encourages us to embrace challenges, learn from our mistakes, and seek out new opportunities for growth. In contrast, a fixed mindset may lead us to avoid challenges and shy away from learning opportunities, limiting our potential for growth and development.

Mindset can help us overcome obstacles: A growth mindset can help us overcome obstacles and setbacks more effectively. By viewing challenges as opportunities for growth and learning, we can approach them with a positive and resilient mindset, which can help us find solutions and make progress towards our goals.

Mindset impacts our self-esteem: Our mindset can also impact our self-esteem and sense of self-worth. A growth mindset encourages us to focus on our effort, progress, and potential, rather than our fixed traits or abilities. This can lead to greater self-confidence, resilience, and a more positive self-image.

Mindset can foster innovation: A growth mindset encourages us to explore new ideas, take risks, and challenge the status quo. This mindset can foster innovation in our personal and professional lives, leading to new discoveries, products, and services that can benefit society as a whole.

Mindset affects our relationships: Our mindset can have a significant impact on our relationships with others. A growth mindset encourages us to be open-minded, empathetic, and understanding, which can lead to stronger and more positive relationships. In contrast, a fixed mindset may cause us to judge and criticize others, leading to conflict and strained relationships.

Mindset can help us adapt to change: A growth mindset can help us adapt to change more effectively. By viewing change as an opportunity for growth and learning, we can approach it with a positive and curious mindset, which can help us navigate uncertainty and make the most of new opportunities.

Mindset can lead to greater happiness: A growth mindset can lead to greater happiness and life satisfaction. By focusing on the process of learning and growth, rather than fixed outcomes, we can cultivate a sense of purpose and meaning in our lives, which can contribute to our overall well-being.

Mindset can promote diversity and inclusion: A growth mindset can help us embrace diversity and promote inclusion in our personal and professional lives. By valuing and respecting different perspectives and experiences, we can build more inclusive and supportive communities that benefit everyone.

In conclusion, mindset matters because it can impact our relationships, ability to adapt to change, happiness, and efforts to promote diversity and inclusion. By cultivating a growth mindset, we can become more resilient, adaptable, and empathetic individuals who are better equipped to navigate the challenges and opportunities of life.

Mindset refers to an individual's attitudes, beliefs, and thought patterns. It is the lens through which an individual views and interprets the world around them. Mindset can influence how individuals approach challenges, cope with setbacks, and make decisions.

There are two main types of mindset: **Fixed Mindset and Growth Mindset.**

A fixed mindset is characterized by the belief that one's abilities and traits are fixed and cannot be changed. Individuals with a fixed mindset may avoid challenges, give up easily in the face of setbacks, and feel threatened by the success of others. They may believe that talent alone is the key to success and that effort is not important.

On the other hand, a growth mindset is characterized by the belief that one's abilities and traits can be developed through hard work and dedication. Individuals with a growth mindset embrace challenges, persist in the face of setbacks, and see the success of others as a source of inspiration and motivation. They believe that effort and perseverance are key factors in achieving success.

It is important to note that mindset is not necessarily fixed, and individuals can develop a growth mindset through intentional effort and practice. By adopting a growth mindset, individuals can increase their resilience, creativity, and ability to learn and adapt to new situations.

In addition to fixed and growth mindsets, there are also other types of mindsets that have been identified. Here are a few examples:

Abundance mindset: This is the belief that there are plenty of opportunities and resources available to everyone, and that success is not a zero-sum game. Individuals with an abundance mindset tend to be more generous and collaborative, and they view setbacks as opportunities for growth and learning.

Scarcity mindset: This is the belief that resources are limited and that one must compete with others to succeed. Individuals with a scarcity mindset may feel anxious or threatened by competition, and they may be more likely to engage in unethical behaviors in order to get ahead.

Fixed trait mindset: This is the belief that one's personality traits are fixed and unchangeable. For example, someone with a fixed trait mindset may believe that they are naturally introverted and therefore unable to become more outgoing. This can lead to a self-fulfilling prophecy, where the individual fails to take actions that could lead to personal growth.

Learning mindset: This is the belief that one can learn and improve through deliberate practice and effort. Individuals with a learning mindset tend to be more open to feedback and willing to try new things, and they view failure as an opportunity to learn and improve.

It's worth noting that mindset can be influenced by a variety of factors, including past experiences, social and cultural norms, and personal beliefs and values. However, with intentional effort and practice, individuals can shift their mindset to one that is more conducive to growth and success.

Mindset can impact behavior: An individual's mindset can have a significant impact on their behavior. For example, someone with a fixed mindset may avoid challenges or give up easily, whereas someone with a growth mindset may be more likely to persist in the face of difficulty and work to overcome obstacles.

Mindset can be developed: While mindset is influenced by a variety of factors, it is not necessarily fixed. With intentional effort and practice, individuals can develop a more growth-oriented mindset. This may involve challenging limiting beliefs, seeking out new experiences, and embracing failure as an opportunity for growth.

Mindset can impact achievement: Studies have shown that mindset can have a significant impact on achievement. Individuals with a growth mindset tend to achieve more over time than those with a fixed mindset, as they are more likely to persist in the face of difficulty and work to improve their skills and abilities.

Mindset can impact well-being: In addition to impacting achievement, mindset can also impact well-being. Individuals with a growth mindset tend to experience less stress and anxiety, as they are more likely to view challenges as opportunities for growth rather than threats to their self-worth.

Mindset can be contagious: Mindset can be contagious, meaning that the beliefs and attitudes of those around us can influence our own mindset. For example, if we surround ourselves with people who have a growth mindset and embrace challenges and learning, we are more likely to adopt those same beliefs and attitudes ourselves.

Mindset can influence relationships: Mindset can also impact our relationships, as individuals with different mindsets may approach interactions and conflicts in different ways. For example, someone with a fixed mindset may be more likely to blame others or become defensive in a conflict, whereas someone with a growth mindset may be more willing to listen and seek out solutions.

Mindset can impact leadership: Mindset can also impact leadership, as leaders with a growth mindset are more likely to foster a culture of learning and development within their organization. They may be more willing to take risks, embrace failure as a learning opportunity, and encourage their team members to do the same.

Mindset can be influenced by language: The language we use can also influence our mindset. For example, using phrases like "I can't" or "I'm not good at" can reinforce a fixed mindset, whereas using phrases like "I haven't learned how to" or "I'm working on improving" can reinforce a growth mindset.

Mindset can impact creativity: Mindset can have a significant impact on creativity. Individuals with a growth mindset tend to be more open to new ideas and approaches, and are more likely to take risks and experiment. This can lead to greater creativity and innovation.

Mindset can impact decision-making: Our mindset can also impact our decision-making. Individuals with a growth mindset tend to approach decisions with an open and curious mindset, and are more likely to seek out information and weigh multiple options before making a decision. This can lead to more informed and effective decision- making.

Mindset can impact learning: Mindset can also impact how we approach learning. Individuals with a growth mindset tend to be more motivated to learn, as they see learning as a way to develop their skills and abilities. They are also more likely to embrace feedback and use it as a tool for improvement.

Mindset can be influenced by social factors: Our mindset can be influenced by the social and cultural factors around us. For example, individuals from cultures that place a high value on effort and hard work may be more likely to have a growth mindset.

Mindset can impact mental health: Finally, mindset can also impact our mental health. Individuals with a growth mindset tend to experience less anxiety and depression, as they are more likely to view challenges and setbacks as opportunities for growth. They are also less likely to engage in negative self-talk or rumination, which can contribute to poor mental health.

Overall, mindset is a powerful factor that can impact many aspects of our lives. By cultivating a growth-oriented mindset, we can increase our resilience, creativity, and ability to learn and adapt to new situations.

Fixed mindset and **growth mindset a**re two different beliefs people have about their abilities and potential. A fixed mindset refers to the belief that one's abilities and traits are fixed and cannot be changed significantly, while a growth mindset refers to the belief that one's abilities and traits can be developed and improved with effort and practice.

Here are some characteristics of both mindsets:

Fixed Mindset:

1. Believes that talent and intelligence are innate and cannot be improved significantly
2. Avoids challenges and risks because failure is seen as a reflection of their abilities
3. Views criticism as constructive feedback and uses it to improve
4. Persists through obstacles and setbacks, seeing them as opportunities to learn and improve
5. Seeks out learning opportunities and welcomes new perspectives and ideas
6. Tends to experience less anxiety and stress because they focus on the process of learning and improving, rather than proving themselves.

It's important to note that most people have a mix of both mindsets in different areas of their lives, and that a growth mindset can be developed with deliberate effort and practice.

Fixed Mindset:

1. May believe that their abilities and success are determined by factors outside of their control, such as luck or social status

2. May feel threatened by the success of others, as it may challenge their belief in their own abilities
3. May avoid seeking help or support because it may be seen as a sign of weakness or incompetence
4. May have a tendency to blame external factors for their failures, rather than taking responsibility and learning from them
5. May focus on short-term goals and immediate gratification, rather than long-term growth and development Growth mindset.
6. Sees failure as an opportunity to learn and improve, rather than a reflection of their abilities
7. Believes that effort and hard work are the key to success, rather than innate talent or intelligence
8. Seeks out challenges and opportunities to learn and grow, even if they are initially outside their comfort zone
9. Is open to feedback and willing to learn from others, even if it means admitting mistakes or weaknesses
10. Has a long-term perspective and is willing to invest time and effort in pursuing their goals and dreams

It's worth noting that having a growth mindset doesn't mean that someone will always succeed or that they won't experience setbacks or failures. However, it does mean that they are more likely to persist through challenges, learn from their mistakes, and ultimately achieve their goals.

Fixed Mindset:

1. May focus on proving themselves and their abilities to others, rather than focusing on their own growth and development
2. May feel threatened by challenges or obstacles, as they see them as a sign of their own limitations
3. May avoid trying new things or taking risks, as they fear failure or looking foolish
4. May have a tendency to give up easily or become discouraged when things don't go according to plan
5. May have a narrow view of success, believing that it is tied to achieving specific outcomes or goals Growth mindset:
6. Sees challenges and obstacles as opportunities for growth and development
7. Embraces the process of learning and is motivated by the pursuit of knowledge and self-improvement
8. Is willing to take risks and try new things, even if they may initially fail or make mistakes
9. Is persistent and resilient in the face of setbacks and obstacles, using them as learning opportunities
10. Has a broad view of success, seeing it as a journey and process rather than a specific outcome or achievement

Fixed Mindset:

1. May feel that their abilities are set in stone and cannot change, leading to a lack of motivation to improve or develop new skills
2. May view setbacks or failures as evidence that they lack natural talent or ability, leading to a fear of taking on new

challenges or risk

3. May be more likely to compare themselves to others rather than focusing on their own growth and progress
4. May be more likely to give up on tasks that they do not excel at quickly, rather than working through challenges and difficulties

Growth Mindset:

1. Sees effort and hard work as the key to success, rather than relying solely on natural talent or ability
2. Believes that their abilities can be developed over time through dedication and practice, leading to a willingness to take on new challenges and expand their skillset
3. Is more likely to focus on their own progress and growth rather than comparing themselves to others
4. Is more likely to persist through challenges and setbacks, viewing them as opportunities for learning and improvement

Overall, adopting a growth mindset can lead to a more positive outlook on personal development and a willingness to take on new challenges. By contrast, a fixed mindset may limit personal growth and development and lead to a fear of taking risks or trying new things.

Fixed Mindset:

1. May have a tendency to avoid feedback or constructive criticism, as it may be seen as an attack on their abilities or intelligence

2. May be more likely to blame external factors for their failures or shortcomings, rather than taking responsibility and looking for ways to improve
3. May be more likely to give up when faced with a difficult challenge or setback, rather than persisting and seeing it as an opportunity for growth
4. May view success as something that is either achieved or not, rather than a process of ongoing improvement and growth

Growth Mindset:

1. Seeks out feedback and constructive criticism as a way to learn and improve, seeing it as an opportunity for growth rather than a threat to their self-esteem
2. Takes responsibility for their failures and shortcomings, using them as a way to learn and improve for the future
3. Views challenges and setbacks as opportunities for growth and learning, persisting through difficulties and seeing them as a chance to develop new skills and abilities
4. Sees success as a journey of ongoing improvement and growth, rather than a fixed state that is either achieved or not.

Improved learning and performance: People with a growth mindset believe that their abilities can be developed through hard work and dedication. As a result, they are more likely to embrace challenges and persist in the face of obstacles, leading to improved learning and performance over time.

Increased resilience and adaptability: A growth mindset helps people to view setbacks and failures as opportunities for growth and learning, rather than as signs of inadequacy or defeat. This mindset can increase resilience and adaptability in the face of challenges, both in personal and professional contexts.

Greater creativity and innovation: When people believe that their abilities can be developed, they are more likely to take risks and explore new ideas. This openness to experimentation and learning can lead to greater creativity and innovation.

Greater motivation and engagement: People with a growth mindset tend to be more motivated and engaged in their work and other pursuits. They see challenges as opportunities to learn and grow, which gives them a sense of purpose and direction.

Improved relationships: Adopting a growth mindset can also improve relationships with others. People with a growth mindset are more likely to be open to feedback and willing to learn from others. This can lead to better communication, collaboration, and teamwork.

Reduced anxiety and stress: When people believe that their abilities can improve with effort, they are less likely to feel anxious or stressed about their performance. This can lead to greater emotional well-being and a more positive outlook on life.

Greater sense of self-efficacy: A growth mindset can also increase a person's sense of self-efficacy, or belief in their ability to achieve their goals. This can lead to greater confidence, resilience, and a willingness to take on new challenges.

Increased focus on effort and learning: People with a growth mindset tend to focus more on the process of learning and effort, rather than just the outcome. This can help them to develop a more positive attitude towards challenges and setbacks, and to embrace the learning process as a valuable experience in itself.

Greater willingness to seek out feedback: People with a growth mindset are often more willing to seek out feedback from others, even if it may be critical or uncomfortable. This can help them to identify areas for improvement and to continue growing and developing over time.

Improved decision-making: A growth mindset can also lead to more effective decision-making. People with a growth mindset tend to be more open-minded and willing to consider different perspectives and options. This can help them to make more informed decisions and to be more adaptable in changing circumstances.

Enhanced problem-solving skills: When people approach challenges with a growth mindset, they are more likely to be creative and resourceful in finding solutions. This can lead to enhanced problem-solving skills and a greater ability to overcome obstacles.

Better academic and career outcomes: Finally, research has shown that students who adopt a growth mindset tend to achieve better academic outcomes, such as higher grades and test scores. Similarly, employees with a growth mindset may be more successful in their careers, as they are more willing to take on new challenges and develop new skills.

Increased empathy and understanding: People with a growth mindset tend to be more empathetic and understanding towards others. They recognize that everyone has the potential for growth and development, and are more likely to be patient and supportive of others as they work to overcome challenges.

Improved health and well-being: There is evidence to suggest that adopting a growth mindset can have positive effects on physical and mental health. For example, studies have shown that people with a growth mindset may be more likely to engage in healthy behaviors like exercise and nutrition, and may experience lower levels of stress and anxiety.

Greater sense of purpose and meaning: Finally, a growth mindset can help people to develop a greater sense of purpose and meaning in their lives. By embracing challenges and seeking out opportunities for growth and development, people can cultivate a sense of personal fulfillment and satisfaction.

Greater self-awareness: People with a growth mindset tend to be more self-aware, as they are constantly reflecting on their experiences and seeking out opportunities for growth and development. This can help them to identify their strengths and weaknesses, and to make more informed decisions about their personal and professional lives.

Increased innovation and entrepreneurship: A growth mindset can be particularly beneficial for entrepreneurs and innovators, as it encourages people to take risks and pursue new ideas. By embracing failure as a learning opportunity, entrepreneurs and innovators can develop a more experimental and creative approach to problem-solving.

Improved leadership skills: Leaders who adopt a growth mindset tend to be more effective and inspiring, as they encourage their team members to embrace challenges and pursue growth and development. By modeling a growth mindset, leaders can create a culture of innovation and continuous improvement within their organizations.

Enhanced sense of community and connection: Finally, a growth mindset can help people to develop a greater sense of community and connection with others. By embracing challenges and seeking out opportunities for growth and development, people can develop a sense of shared purpose and connection with others who are on a similar journey.

In summary, a growth mindset can have a wide range of benefits, from increased self-awareness and innovation to improved leadership skills and a greater sense of community and connection. It is a powerful tool for personal and professional growth, and can help people to achieve their full potential in all areas of their lives.

Having a fixed mindset means believing that your abilities and intelligence are set in stone and cannot be changed. In contrast, a growth mindset is the belief that your abilities and intelligence can be developed through hard work, dedication, and a willingness to learn and improve.

Overcoming a fixed mindset requires recognizing when you have a fixed mindset, challenging your fixed beliefs, and adopting a growth mindset.

The first step is to recognize when you have a fixed mindset. This can be challenging because fixed beliefs often feel true and accurate. However, some signs of a fixed mindset include avoiding challenges, giving up easily, feeling threatened by the success of others, and believing that talent is the most important factor for success.

Once you recognize that you have a fixed mindset, the next step is to challenge your fixed beliefs. This involves questioning the beliefs that are holding you back and looking for evidence that contradicts them. For example, if you believe that you are not good at math and never will be, challenge that belief by looking for examples of people who have struggled with math but have ultimately succeeded through hard work and perseverance.

Finally, adopting a growth mindset means embracing the idea that your abilities can be developed through dedication and effort. This involves focusing on learning and improvement rather than just on outcomes or talent. It also means being open to feedback, learning from mistakes, and embracing challenges as opportunities to learn and grow.

Embrace challenges: Instead of avoiding challenges, seek them out as opportunities to learn and grow. This can help you develop new skills and build confidence in your abilities.

Learn from mistakes: Rather than seeing mistakes as failures, view them as opportunities to learn and improve. Analyze what went wrong and what you can do differently next time.

Focus on effort: Instead of focusing solely on outcomes, focus on the effort you put into achieving those outcomes. Acknowledge and celebrate your hard work and progress along the way.

Cultivate a love of learning: View learning as a lifelong journey, not just something you do in school. Seek out new information and experiences that challenge and inspire you.

Surround yourself with growth-minded people: Surrounding yourself with people who have a growth mindset can help reinforce your own growth mindset. Seek out friends, colleagues, and mentors who encourage and support your growth and development.

Believe in your potential: Start by believing that you have the potential to learn and grow. Instead of thinking "I can't do it," try thinking "I can't do it yet, but I'm willing to try and learn."

Practice self-compassion: Recognize that everyone, including yourself, makes mistakes and experiences setbacks. Be kind and compassionate towards yourself when things don't go as planned.

Visualize success: Visualize yourself achieving your goals and succeeding in the areas where you want to grow. This can help you build confidence and motivation.

Learn from others: Seek out role models and mentors who embody a growth mindset. Look for people who have overcome challenges and achieved success through hard work and dedication.

Celebrate progress: Celebrate your progress and accomplishments, no matter how small they may seem. This can help you stay motivated and build momentum towards your goals.

Challenge negative self-talk: Notice when you are engaging in negative self-talk, such as "I'm not good enough" or "I'll never be able to do this." Challenge these thoughts by asking yourself if they are really true, and look for evidence that contradicts them.

Embrace feedback: Seek out feedback from others, and view it as an opportunity to learn and improve. Be open to constructive criticism, and use it to make adjustments and improvements.

Set realistic goals: Set goals that are challenging but achievable, and break them down into smaller, manageable steps. This can help you stay motivated and build momentum towards your larger goals.

Be persistent: Persistence is key to developing a growth mindset. Don't give up when things get tough, and keep working towards your goals even when progress seems slow.

Practice gratitude: Cultivate a sense of gratitude for the opportunities and resources you have, and focus on the positive aspects of your life. This can help you stay motivated and optimistic even in the face of challenges.

Stay curious: Cultivate a sense of curiosity about the world around you, and seek out new experiences and information. This can help you stay engaged and motivated, and can open up new opportunities for learning and growth.

Take risks: Don't be afraid to take calculated risks and step outside of your comfort zone. This can help you learn new skills and gain valuable experience, and can also help you build confidence in your abilities.

Practice mindfulness: Mindfulness can help you stay present and focused, and can also help you cultivate a more positive and growth-oriented mindset. Try practicing mindfulness meditation or other mindfulness techniques to help you stay centered and focused.

Embrace failure: Failure is a natural part of the learning process. Instead of seeing failure as a negative, view it as an opportunity to learn and grow. Take the lessons you learn from your failures and use them to make improvements and adjustments.

Surround yourself with positivity: Surround yourself with positive people and environments that support your growth mindset. Seek out people who encourage and inspire you, and avoid negativity and criticism that can bring you down.

Remember, adopting a growth mindset is a journey, not a destination. It takes time, effort, and practice to develop a mindset that will help you achieve your goals and reach your full potential. Be patient with yourself, and keep working towards a more growth-oriented mindset.

There is a strong relationship between mindset and success, achievement, goal setting, and perseverance. Your mindset, or the way you think about yourself and the world around you, can have a significant impact on your ability to achieve your goals and succeed in life.

Individuals with a growth mindset, for example, believe that their abilities and intelligence can be developed through hard work and dedication. This mindset can be particularly beneficial when it comes to achieving goals and persevering through challenges, as it fosters a belief in one's ability to improve and overcome obstacles.

In contrast, individuals with a fixed mindset believe that their abilities and intelligence are set in stone and cannot be changed. This mindset can limit one's potential for growth and achievement, as it can lead to a fear of failure and a lack of resilience in the face of setbacks.

Research has shown that individuals with a growth mindset tend to be more successful in a variety of domains, including academics, sports, and business. They are more likely to set challenging goals for themselves and persist in the face of obstacles, leading to greater achievement and success over time.

Mindset and Success: As mentioned earlier, mindset can have a significant impact on one's ability to succeed. Individuals with a growth mindset tend to view challenges as opportunities for growth and learning, while those with a fixed mindset may view challenges as threats to their abilities. This can lead to different responses to setbacks and failures, with those with a growth mindset being more likely to rebound and try again.

Mindset and Achievement: Mindset can also influence achievement by shaping the goals we set for ourselves. Individuals with a growth mindset tend to set more challenging goals for themselves, as they believe that their abilities can be developed through effort and practice. This can lead to greater achievement over time, as individuals with a growth mindset are more likely to push themselves to improve and excel.

Mindset and Goal Setting: The way we approach goal setting can also be influenced by our mindset. Individuals with a growth mindset tend to set goals that are focused on learning and improvement, while those with a fixed mindset may be more focused on proving their abilities or avoiding failure. This can impact the types of goals we set for ourselves and how we approach achieving them.

Mindset and Perseverance: Finally, mindset can impact our ability to persevere through challenges and setbacks. Individuals with a growth mindset tend to be more resilient in the face of adversity, as they view challenges as opportunities for growth and learning. This can help them to stay motivated and persist in the face of obstacles, leading to greater success and achievement over time.

Mindset and Creativity: A growth mindset can also impact creativity, as it encourages individuals to explore new ideas and take risks. Individuals with a growth mindset may be more willing to try new approaches or experiment with different solutions, which can lead to greater creativity and innovation.

Mindset and Leadership: Mindset can also play a role in effective leadership. Leaders with a growth mindset tend to be more adaptable and open to feedback, which can help them to continuously improve and develop their skills.

They may also be better equipped to handle challenges and setbacks, as they view them as opportunities for growth and learning.

Mindset and Learning: Finally, mindset can impact how we approach learning. Individuals with a growth mindset tend to be more engaged and motivated in the learning process, as they view it as an opportunity to develop their abilities. They may also be more willing to seek out feedback and take on new challenges, which can lead to greater learning and growth over time.

Mindset and Relationships: Our mindset can also impact our relationships with others. Individuals with a growth mindset tend to be more open to feedback and willing to work on themselves, which can lead to healthier and more productive relationships. They may also be better equipped to handle conflicts and challenges, as they view them as opportunities to learn and grow.

Mindset and Confidence: Mindset can also impact our levels of confidence and self-belief. Individuals with a growth mindset tend to have higher levels of self-efficacy, or the belief in their ability to succeed. This can lead to greater confidence and motivation, as they are more likely to take on new challenges and persist through setbacks.

Mindset and Resilience: Resilience, or the ability to bounce back from setbacks, is a key factor in achieving success. Individuals with a growth mindset tend to be more resilient, as they view setbacks as temporary and solvable. They may also be more likely to seek out support and resources to help them overcome challenges.

Mindset and Motivation: Finally, mindset can impact our levels of motivation and engagement. Individuals with a growth mindset tend to be more motivated and engaged in their pursuits, as they view them as opportunities to learn and grow. They may also be more likely to set ambitious goals and work towards them consistently over time.

Mindset and Decision Making: Our mindset can also impact how we make decisions. Individuals with a growth mindset tend to be more open-minded and willing to consider multiple perspectives when making decisions. This can lead to more informed and effective decision-making, as they are able to weigh the pros and cons of different options.

Mindset and Innovation: A growth mindset can also foster innovation and creativity. Individuals with a growth mindset are more likely to take risks and try new things, which can lead to new ideas and breakthroughs. They may also be more willing to challenge the status quo and think outside the box.

Mindset and Adaptability: The ability to adapt to changing circumstances is becoming increasingly important in today's rapidly changing world. Individuals with a growth mindset tend to be more adaptable, as they view change as an opportunity to learn and grow. They may also be more willing to embrace new technologies and ways of working.

Mindset and Mental Health: Finally, mindset can impact our mental health and well-being. Individuals with a growth mindset tend to have more positive self-talk and beliefs, which can lead to lower levels of stress and anxiety. They may also be more likely to seek out support and resources when needed, as they view challenges as solvable.

In conclusion, mindset is a powerful predictor of success, achievement, and well-being. By cultivating a growth mindset and focusing on learning and improvement, individuals can develop the resilience and adaptability needed to thrive in today's rapidly changing world.

The power of **positive thinking** is a concept that has been around for centuries, but it has gained more attention in recent years due to the growing body of scientific research that supports its effectiveness. Positive thinking is a mindset that involves focusing on the good in any situation and expecting positive outcomes. It is not a magical solution to all of life's problems, but it can certainly help to improve one's overall well-being and outlook on life.

The science of positive thinking has shown that our thoughts and beliefs have a significant impact on our emotions, behaviors, and ultimately, our outcomes. When we focus on positive thoughts and beliefs, we are more likely to experience positive emotions such as happiness, joy, and contentment. These positive emotions can lead to positive behaviors such as being more productive, creative, and motivated to pursue our goals.

Research has also shown that positive thinking can have physical health benefits. People who practice positive thinking have been found to have lower levels of stress, improved immune function, and reduced risk of chronic diseases such as heart disease and diabetes. Positive thinking can also help to improve relationships, as it promotes empathy, compassion, and forgiveness.

So, what are some strategies for developing positive thinking? One approach is to practice gratitude. This involves focusing on what we are thankful for in our lives and expressing appreciation for those things. Another strategy is to reframe negative thoughts into positive ones. Instead of dwelling on what went wrong, we can focus on what we learned from the experience and how we can improve in the future. Positive self-talk is also an effective strategy for developing positive thinking. This involves replacing negative self-talk with positive affirmations such as "I am capable" or "I am worthy."

There are many benefits to adopting a positive thinking mindset. One of the most significant benefits is improved mental health. People who practice positive thinking are less likely to experience depression, anxiety, and other mental health issues. This is because positive thinking helps to reduce stress, increase resilience, and promote a sense of well-being.

Another benefit of positive thinking is increased motivation. When we focus on positive thoughts and beliefs, we are more likely to be motivated to pursue our goals. This is because positive thinking helps to increase our confidence, optimism, and sense of purpose. When we believe in ourselves and our abilities, we are more likely to take risks and pursue our dreams.

Positive thinking can also improve our relationships with others. When we focus on positive thoughts and beliefs, we are more likely to be kind, compassionate, and empathetic towards others. This helps to strengthen our relationships and build trust and respect with others.

Finally, positive thinking can help us to cope with difficult situations. When we face challenges and setbacks, positive thinking helps us to stay focused on solutions rather than problems. It helps us to see opportunities rather than obstacles, and to maintain a sense of hope and optimism even in the face of adversity.

In order to develop a positive thinking mindset, it is important to practice self-awareness. This involves paying attention to our thoughts and beliefs and identifying any negative patterns or biases. Once we are aware of these negative patterns, we can begin to reframe them into positive ones.

Another strategy for developing positive thinking is to surround ourselves with positive people and influences. This can include reading positive books, listening to uplifting music, and spending time with people who have a positive outlook on life.

One of the key components of positive thinking is mindfulness. Mindfulness involves being present in the moment and fully engaged with our thoughts, emotions, and surroundings. When we practice mindfulness, we are less likely to get caught up in negative thoughts and emotions, and more likely to focus on the positive aspects of our lives.

Another effective strategy for developing positive thinking is to set goals and visualize success. When we set clear goals and visualize ourselves achieving them, we create a positive mindset that helps us to stay motivated and focused on our goals. Visualization is a powerful tool that can help us to overcome obstacles and stay positive in the face of adversity.

It is also important to practice self-compassion when developing a positive thinking mindset. Self-compassion involves being kind and understanding towards ourselves, even when we make mistakes or experience setbacks. When we practice self-compassion, we are less likely to be self-critical or judgmental, and more likely to focus on our strengths and positive qualities.

Finally, it is important to practice gratitude on a regular basis. This involves focusing on the positive aspects of our lives and expressing gratitude for them. Gratitude helps us to stay positive and optimistic, even in the face of challenges or difficulties. By focusing on the good in our lives, we can develop a positive mindset that helps us to overcome obstacles and achieve our goals.

Positive thinking can also have a significant impact on our physical health. Studies have shown that people who practice positive thinking have lower levels of stress hormones, such as cortisol, which can contribute to chronic health problems such as heart disease, diabetes, and obesity. Positive thinking has also been linked to stronger immune function, which can help to prevent illness and disease.

Another benefit of positive thinking is improved creativity and problem-solving skills. When we are in a positive mindset, we are more likely to be open to new ideas and solutions. This can lead to increased creativity and innovation, as well as better problem-solving skills.

Positive thinking can also improve our self-esteem and confidence. When we focus on our strengths and positive qualities, we are more likely to feel good about ourselves and our abilities. This can lead to improved self-esteem and self-confidence, which can have a positive impact on all areas of our lives.

To develop a positive thinking mindset, it is important to practice self-reflection and self-awareness. This involves paying attention to our thoughts and beliefs, and identifying any negative patterns or biases. Once we are aware of these negative patterns, we can begin to reframe them into positive ones.

It is also important to surround ourselves with positive people and influences. This can include reading positive books, watching uplifting movies, and spending time with people who have a positive outlook on life.

Finally, it is important to practice self-care and stress management techniques. This can include regular exercise, meditation, and mindfulness practices. By taking care of our physical and mental health, we can improve our overall well-being and develop a positive thinking mindset that helps us to achieve our goals and live our best lives.

Mindset and self-esteem are closely related concepts. Mindset refers to the set of attitudes and beliefs that shape how we perceive and respond to the world around us. Self-esteem, on the other hand, refers to our overall sense of self- worth and confidence in our abilities.

The way we think about ourselves and our abilities can have a significant impact on our self-esteem. People with a growth mindset, which is the belief that our abilities can be developed through hard work and dedication, tend to have higher self-esteem than those with a fixed mindset, which is the belief that our abilities are innate and cannot be changed.

There are several strategies that can help build self-esteem, including:

1. **Practice self-compassion:** Be kind and understanding toward yourself. Recognize that everyone makes mistakes and that it's okay to fail.
2. **Challenge negative self-talk:** Pay attention to the way you talk to yourself and try to reframe negative self-talk into more positive and realistic statements.
3. **Set achievable goals:** Set goals that are challenging but realistic, and work towards them step by step.
4. **Celebrate your accomplishments**: Take time to acknowledge and celebrate your achievements, no matter how small they may seem.
5. **Surround yourself with positivity:** Surround yourself with people who uplift and support you, and engage in activities that make you feel good about yourself.
6. **Practice self-care:** Take care of your physical, emotional, and mental health by getting enough sleep, eating well, exercising, and practicing relaxation techniques.

7. **Focus on your strengths:** Identify your unique strengths and talents, and focus on developing them. This can help you feel more confident and capable in areas where you excel.
8. **Take risks:** Challenge yourself to step outside of your comfort zone and take on new challenges. This can help you build confidence in your ability to handle new situations and overcome obstacles.
9. **Practice gratitude:** Take time each day to reflect on the things you are grateful for in your life. This can help you cultivate a more positive outlook and boost your overall sense of well-being.
10. **Learn from setbacks:** Instead of getting discouraged by setbacks or failures, use them as opportunities to learn and grow. Reflect on what went wrong and what you can do differently next time.
11. **Practice assertiveness:** Being assertive means standing up for yourself and expressing your needs and opinions in a respectful and confident way. Practicing assertiveness can help you feel more in control and confident in your interactions with others.
12. **Seek professional help if needed:** If you are struggling with low self-esteem or other mental health issues, seek professional help from a therapist or counselor. They can provide you with additional tools and strategies for building self-esteem and improving your overall well-being.
13. **Practice self-acceptance:** Accept yourself for who you are, flaws and all. Remember that nobody is perfect, and it's okay to have weaknesses.
14. **Avoid comparisons:** Try to avoid comparing yourself to others, as this can lead to feelings of inadequacy and low

self-esteem. Instead, focus on your own progress and accomplishments.

15. **Volunteer or help others:** Helping others can boost your sense of purpose and self-worth. Look for volunteer opportunities in your community or find ways to help friends and family members in need.
16. **Take care of your appearance:** While appearance isn't everything, taking care of your physical appearance can help boost your confidence and self-esteem. This might include things like grooming, dressing in clothes that make you feel good, or exercising to improve your physical health.
17. **Practice positive self-talk:** Pay attention to the way you talk to yourself, and try to replace negative self-talk with positive affirmations. For example, instead of saying "I can't do this," try saying "I'm capable of learning and growing."
18. **Keep a journal:** Writing down your thoughts and feelings can help you process your emotions and gain insight into your patterns of thinking. Try keeping a daily journal to reflect on your experiences and track your progress.
19. **Practice mindfulness:** Mindfulness involves paying attention to the present moment without judgment. Practicing mindfulness can help you become more aware of your thoughts and feelings, and learn to accept them without getting caught up in negative patterns of thinking.
20. **Set healthy boundaries:** Setting healthy boundaries involves knowing your limits and communicating them to others in a clear and assertive way. This can help you feel more in control and respected in your relationships with others.
21. **Learn new skills:** Learning new skills or taking up new hobbies can help you feel more confident and capable. Look

for opportunities to learn and grow, whether it's taking a class, joining a club, or trying something new.

22. **Practice self-forgiveness:** It's important to forgive yourself for past mistakes or shortcomings. Remember that everyone makes mistakes, and use these experiences as opportunities for growth and learning.

23. **Focus on the positive:** Instead of dwelling on your weaknesses or failures, try to focus on your strengths and accomplishments. Celebrate your successes, no matter how small they may seem.

24. **Develop a support network:** Surround yourself with positive, supportive people who encourage and uplift you. This can help you build a sense of community and help boost your self-esteem.

25. **Practice self-compassion:** Treat yourself with the same kindness and understanding that you would offer to a good friend. Be gentle with yourself, and remember that it's okay to make mistakes or struggle with certain things.

26. **Practice gratitude:** Take time each day to reflect on the things you are grateful for in your life. This can help you cultivate a more positive outlook and boost your overall sense of well-being.

27. **Challenge negative beliefs:** Pay attention to negative beliefs or self-talk that may be holding you back, and challenge them with more positive and realistic alternatives.

28. **Take care of your body**: Taking care of your physical health can have a positive impact on your self-esteem. Make sure to eat a balanced diet, get enough sleep, and engage in regular exercise.

29. **Find meaning and purpose:** Identifying your values and finding meaning and purpose in your life can help boost

your sense of self-worth. Consider what gives your life meaning and work towards incorporating those things into your daily life.

30. **Celebrate progress, not just perfection:** Instead of focusing solely on achieving perfection, celebrate progress and growth along the way. Recognize that progress can come in small steps, and each step is worth celebrating.

Remember, building self-esteem is an ongoing process that requires patience, commitment, and self-compassion. Try incorporating these strategies into your daily life, and don't be afraid to seek help or support if you need it.

Mindset plays a significant role in the quality of our **relationships**. Our mindset, or our beliefs and attitudes about ourselves and the world around us, can influence how we interact with others, how we perceive their actions, and how we respond to them.

A negative mindset, for example, can lead to a lack of trust, defensiveness, and a tendency to focus on problems rather than solutions. On the other hand, a positive mindset can foster openness, empathy, and a willingness to work through challenges together.

Here are some strategies for cultivating a positive mindset and improving your relationships:

Practice gratitude: Focus on what you appreciate about the people in your life and express your thanks to them. This can help shift your focus from negative to positive aspects of your relationships.

Cultivate empathy: Try to understand another person's perspective, even if you don't agree with it. This can help you communicate more effectively and build stronger connections.

Practice active listening: Listening attentively to others can help them feel heard and understood, which can strengthen your relationship.

Develop a growth mindset: Believe that your relationships can improve and that challenges can be overcome through effort and learning. This can help you approach your relationships with a positive attitude and a willingness to work through difficulties.

Practice self-care: Taking care of your own physical and emotional needs can help you approach your relationships with a more positive and resilient mindset.

Focus on strengths: Instead of dwelling on weaknesses or negative aspects of your relationships, try to focus on the strengths and positive qualities of the people in your life. This can help you appreciate and value them more.

Practice forgiveness: Holding grudges or refusing to forgive can create resentment and strain in your relationships. Practice forgiveness, both for yourself and others, to promote healing and strengthen your connections.

Communicate effectively: Good communication is key to healthy relationships. Be clear and direct in your communication, listen actively, and try to understand the other person's perspective.

Set boundaries: Setting healthy boundaries can help you maintain a positive mindset and prevent negative interactions or behaviors from affecting your relationships.

Practice self-reflection: Regularly reflect on your thoughts, feelings, and behaviors in your relationships. This can help you identify areas for improvement and make positive changes.

Practice mindfulness: Mindfulness can help you stay present and attuned to your thoughts and emotions, leading to more intentional and positive interactions with others.

Practice self-compassion: Treat yourself with kindness and understanding, just as you would a friend. This can help you cultivate a more positive and compassionate mindset, which can in turn improve your relationships.

Celebrate successes: Celebrate your own and others' successes, no matter how small. This can help create positive energy and foster a sense of connection and support.

Avoid negative self-talk: Negative self-talk can erode your self-confidence and affect your relationships. Practice positive self-talk and focus on your strengths and accomplishments.

Seek support: Don't be afraid to seek support from friends, family, or a therapist. Having a support system can help you maintain a positive mindset and navigate challenges in your relationships.

Learn conflict resolution skills: Conflict is a natural part of relationships, but it can be a source of stress and tension if not handled properly. Learning conflict resolution skills such as active listening, compromise, and problem- solving can help you approach conflicts in a positive and constructive way.

Practice gratitude journaling: Writing down things you're grateful for can help you cultivate a positive mindset and focus on the positive aspects of your relationships. Try writing down three things you're grateful for each day.

Be authentic: Being true to yourself and expressing your authentic thoughts and feelings can help you build deeper and more meaningful connections with others.

Practice optimism: Believe that things will work out for the best, even in difficult situations. This can help you approach challenges with a positive and hopeful attitude.

Practice patience: Developing stronger relationships takes time and effort. Practice patience and be willing to invest the time and energy needed to build deeper connections with others.

Remember, having a positive mindset is not about being perfect or always having a positive attitude. It's about approaching your relationships with a constructive and growth-oriented mindset, and being willing to learn and grow together with others. With time and practice, these strategies can help you cultivate stronger, healthier, and more fulfilling relationships.

The connection between **mindset and health** is a powerful one, and there is growing evidence to suggest that our mental and emotional states can have a profound impact on our physical health and well-being. The mind-body connection refers to the idea that our thoughts, feelings, and attitudes can influence the function of our body's physiological systems, including the immune system, cardiovascular system, and nervous system.

Research has shown that a positive mindset can improve immune function, reduce the risk of chronic disease, and even increase lifespan. On the other hand, chronic stress, anxiety, and negative emotions have been linked to a range of physical health problems, including cardiovascular disease, digestive disorders, and chronic pain.

To improve our health and well-being, it's important to cultivate a positive mindset and adopt healthy strategies that support both our mental and physical health. Here are a few strategies that can help:

Practice mindfulness: Mindfulness is a practice that involves being present in the moment and paying attention to our thoughts, feelings, and physical sensations without judgment. Research has shown that mindfulness can reduce stress, improve mood, and even lower blood pressure.

Exercise regularly: Exercise is not only good for our physical health, but it's also been shown to improve mood, reduce stress, and boost our overall sense of well-being.

Get enough sleep: Sleep is crucial for our physical and mental health. Lack of sleep can lead to fatigue, irritability, and even depression. Aim for 7-8 hours of sleep per night to ensure you're getting enough rest.

Connect with others: Social support is important for our mental and emotional well-being. Make time for friends and family, or join a group or club to meet new people with shared interests.

Practice gratitude: Gratitude is the practice of focusing on the positive aspects of our lives and expressing appreciation for the good things we have. Research has shown that gratitude can improve mood, reduce stress, and even boost the immune system.

Eat a healthy diet: Eating a balanced diet that includes plenty of fruits, vegetables, whole grains, and lean protein can help improve overall health and reduce the risk of chronic disease. Aim to eat a variety of nutrient-rich foods and limit processed and sugary foods.

Practice self-care: Self-care refers to the practice of taking time to care for ourselves, both physically and emotionally. This can include activities such as taking a bath, reading a book, or meditating. Prioritizing self-care can help reduce stress and improve overall well-being.

Manage stress: Chronic stress can have a negative impact on both physical and mental health. Finding healthy ways to manage stress, such as through exercise, meditation, or relaxation techniques, can help reduce its impact.

Practice positive self-talk: The way we talk to ourselves can have a big impact on our mental and emotional health. Practicing positive self-talk, such as reminding ourselves of our strengths and accomplishments, can help improve self-esteem and reduce negative self-talk.

Seek professional help when needed: If you're struggling with a mental health issue or chronic health condition, it's important to seek professional help. A therapist, counselor, or healthcare provider can provide guidance and support to help improve your overall health and well-being.

Engage in activities that bring you joy: Doing things that bring you joy and fulfillment can help boost your mood and overall sense of well-being. This can include hobbies, creative pursuits, or spending time in nature.

Practice positive relationships: Building and nurturing positive relationships with others can help improve our mental and emotional health. This can include spending time with loved ones, joining a social group, or volunteering in your community.

Stay hydrated: Drinking enough water is important for maintaining good health. Aim to drink at least 8-10 glasses of water per day, and limit sugary drinks and alcohol.

Take breaks: Taking regular breaks throughout the day can help reduce stress and improve focus. This can include taking a short walk, stretching, or simply stepping away from your work for a few minutes.

Cultivate a growth mindset: A growth mindset involves believing that our abilities and intelligence can be developed over time through hard work and dedication. This can help improve motivation and resilience, and reduce the impact of setbacks and failures.

Practice compassion: Compassion involves showing kindness to ourselves and others, even in difficult situations. Practicing compassion can help improve relationships, reduce stress, and promote feelings of connection and well- being.

Set realistic goals: Setting realistic goals can help improve motivation and provide a sense of purpose. When setting goals, consider breaking them down into smaller, achievable steps to help build momentum and avoid feeling overwhelmed.

Limit screen time: Spending too much time on electronic devices, such as phones, computers, and televisions, can have a negative impact on mental health and sleep. Aim to limit screen time, especially before bed, and engage in other activities, such as reading or meditation, instead.

Practice forgiveness: Holding onto grudges and resentment can have a negative impact on mental health and well- being. Practicing forgiveness, both for yourself and for others, can promote feelings of peace and reduce stress.

Get outside: Spending time in nature has been shown to reduce stress, improve mood, and boost overall well-being. Try to spend time outside each day, even if it's just for a short walk around the block.

Cultivate a sense of purpose: Having a sense of purpose and meaning in life has been linked to improved mental and physical health. Consider volunteering, pursuing a passion project, or engaging in work that aligns with your values.

Remember, improving health and well-being is a journey that requires ongoing effort and commitment. By adopting a holistic approach to health and incorporating a wide range of strategies, you can improve your physical and mental health, build resilience, and live a happier, more fulfilling life.

Mindset plays an important role in **leadership**, as it influences how leaders approach challenges, make decisions, and interact with others. In particular, a growth mindset can be especially beneficial for leaders, as it emphasizes the belief that skills and abilities can be developed through hard work, effort, and persistence.

Here are some strategies for developing a growth mindset as a leader:

Embrace challenges: Leaders with a growth mindset see challenges as opportunities to learn and grow, rather than as threats. They are willing to take on new challenges and are not afraid of failure.

Learn from failure: Failure is an inevitable part of learning and growth. Leaders with a growth mindset see failure as an opportunity to learn, reflect on what went wrong, and identify ways to improve.

Focus on effort and persistence: Leaders with a growth mindset believe that success is a result of hard work, effort, and persistence. They focus on developing their skills and abilities through practice and continuous learning.

Encourage and support others: Leaders with a growth mindset also encourage and support others in their development. They provide feedback, guidance, and opportunities for growth and development.

Emphasize the power of "yet": Leaders with a growth mindset believe that they can learn and improve over time. They use the word "yet" to emphasize that they may not have achieved a goal or mastered a skill yet, but with effort and persistence, they can.

Seek out feedback: Leaders with a growth mindset actively seek out feedback from others to identify areas for improvement. They are open to constructive criticism and use it as an opportunity to learn and grow.

Emphasize the power of "not yet": Leaders with a growth

mindset recognize that they may not have achieved a goal or mastered a skill, but they believe that they can with time and effort. They use the phrase "not yet" to emphasize that they are on a journey of growth and development.

Learn from others: Leaders with a growth mindset recognize that they can learn from others, including their team members, peers, and mentors. They are open to new ideas and perspectives and seek out opportunities to learn from others.

Be adaptable: Leaders with a growth mindset are adaptable and flexible. They recognize that the world is constantly changing, and they are willing to adjust their strategies and approaches as needed.

Practice self-reflection: Leaders with a growth mindset regularly reflect on their experiences, behaviors, and thought patterns. They ask themselves questions such as "What did I learn from this experience?" and "How can I improve for next time?"

By implementing these strategies, leaders can develop a growth mindset that enables them to continuously learn, grow, and improve. This, in turn, can benefit their teams and organizations by fostering a culture of learning and development.

Mindset plays a crucial role in **creativity**, and having a growth mindset can significantly enhance one's creative abilities. A growth mindset is the belief that one's abilities and intelligence can be developed through hard work, dedication, and learning from mistakes, as opposed to a fixed mindset that assumes one's abilities and intelligence are fixed traits that cannot be changed.

Having a growth mindset allows individuals to approach challenges and obstacles with a positive attitude, and see them as opportunities for learning and growth. This perspective can lead to increased creativity because it encourages individuals to take risks, explore new ideas, and experiment with different approaches.

Here are some strategies for developing a creative mindset:

Embrace a growth mindset: Start by recognizing that creativity is not an innate talent that only a select few possess, but rather a skill that can be developed and improved over time. Embrace a growth mindset and believe in your ability to learn and grow creatively.

Cultivate curiosity: Be open to new experiences, ideas, and perspectives. Ask questions, explore new topics, and seek out opportunities to learn and discover new things.

Practice mindfulness: Mindfulness can help you stay present and focused, allowing you to more easily tap into your creative abilities. Try practicing mindfulness meditation, yoga, or other mindfulness techniques.

Experiment: Try new things and don't be afraid to fail. Experiment with different approaches, techniques, and tools to find what works best for you.

Collaborate: Collaborating with others can spark new ideas and perspectives. Seek out opportunities to collaborate with people from different backgrounds and areas of expertise.

Practice divergent thinking: Divergent thinking is the ability to generate multiple solutions or ideas for a single problem. To practice divergent thinking, try brainstorming and coming up with as many ideas as possible, even if they seem unrealistic or impractical. This can help you think outside the box and generate more creative solutions.

Challenge assumptions: Many assumptions we make about the world and ourselves are limiting and can hinder creativity. Challenge these assumptions by asking yourself "why" and "what if" questions. This can help you see things from a different perspective and generate new ideas.

Seek out inspiration: Inspiration can come from anywhere, so make an effort to seek out new sources of inspiration. This could be through reading books, watching movies, listening to music, or exploring nature. Take note of what inspires you and use it to fuel your creative pursuits.

Embrace failure: Failure is an inevitable part of the creative process, but it can also be a valuable learning opportunity. Embrace failure as a chance to learn and grow, and don't be afraid to experiment and take risks.

Practice creativity regularly: Like any skill, creativity requires regular practice. Set aside time each day to engage in creative activities, whether it's writing, painting, or experimenting with new ideas. This can help you develop a creative habit and improve your skills over time.

Practice self-reflection: Take time to reflect on your creative process and the ideas you generate. Ask yourself what worked well and what didn't, and why. This can help you identify patterns and improve your creative process over time.

Engage in diverse experiences: Expose yourself to a variety of experiences and perspectives to expand your thinking and spark new ideas. This could involve traveling, trying new foods, attending cultural events, or simply seeking out different viewpoints.

Find a community: Surround yourself with people who support and encourage your creativity. Join a creative group or find a mentor who can offer feedback and support.

Practice gratitude: Gratitude can help cultivate a positive mindset and increase feelings of happiness and well-being, which can in turn enhance creativity. Take time each day to reflect on what you're grateful for and how it has contributed to your creative process.

Embrace constraints: Constraints can actually enhance creativity by forcing you to think outside the box and find new solutions. Embrace constraints as a challenge and an opportunity to push your creative boundaries.

Practice active listening: Active listening involves fully engaging with others when they speak, asking questions, and seeking to understand their perspectives. By practicing active listening, you can gain new insights and ideas that you might not have considered otherwise.

Embrace ambiguity: Creativity often involves dealing with ambiguity and uncertainty. Rather than feeling overwhelmed or frustrated, try embracing ambiguity as an opportunity to explore new possibilities and generate creative solutions.

Experiment with different environments: Sometimes a change of scenery can help spark creativity. Try working in different environments, such as a coffee shop, park, or library, to see how it affects your creative process.

Learn from others: Seek out mentors, role models, and other creative individuals who inspire you. Look for opportunities to learn from them and incorporate their techniques into your own creative process.

By incorporating these strategies into your life, you can develop a more creative mindset and enhance your ability to generate new ideas, solve problems, and approach challenges with a fresh perspective. Remember that creativity is a skill that can be developed and improved over time, so keep practicing and experimenting to see what works best for you.

Mindset plays a crucial role in **innovation**. An innovative mindset is one that is open to new ideas, curious, and willing to take risks. It is a way of thinking that encourages creativity and problem-solving. Here are some strategies for developing an innovative mindset:

Embrace failure: Failure is a natural part of the innovation process. Embrace it as a learning opportunity and use it to improve your ideas and approach.

Stay curious: Curiosity is the driving force behind innovation. Stay curious about the world around you and always ask questions.

Challenge assumptions: Don't accept things as they are. Challenge assumptions and look for new ways of doing things.

Collaborate: Innovation often requires collaboration. Work with others to generate new ideas and perspectives.

Be adaptable: Innovation requires flexibility and adaptability. Be willing to change course if a new idea or approach presents itself.

Take calculated risks: Innovation often involves taking risks. However, it's important to take calculated risks and weigh the potential outcomes before moving forward.

Practice mindfulness: Being mindful can help you focus and stay present in the moment. This can help you generate new ideas and insights.

Keep learning: Innovation requires continuous learning. Stay informed about new developments in your field and seek out new learning opportunities.

Foster a growth mindset: Believe that your abilities can be developed through hard work, dedication, and perseverance. This will help you approach challenges with a positive and optimistic attitude.

Practice creativity: Creativity is the cornerstone of innovation. Practice creative thinking by engaging in activities like brainstorming, mind mapping, and free writing.

Embrace diversity: Innovation thrives in diverse environments. Seek out diverse perspectives and experiences to broaden your thinking and generate new ideas.

Stay informed: Stay up-to-date on industry trends, emerging technologies, and current events. This will help you identify opportunities for innovation and stay ahead of the curve.

Seek feedback: Feedback is critical for innovation. Seek out feedback from others to help refine your ideas and approach.

Experiment: Try new things and experiment with different approaches. This will help you discover what works and what doesn't, and will ultimately lead to new and innovative solutions.

Stay positive: Innovation can be challenging and frustrating at times. Stay positive and focused on your goals, and remember that every failure is an opportunity to learn and grow.

Adopt a customer-centric approach: Innovation is often driven by a deep understanding of customer needs. Adopt a customer-centric approach by regularly seeking feedback from customers and using their insights to guide your innovation efforts.

Create an innovation-friendly environment: Innovation thrives in an environment that encourages creativity and experimentation. Create a culture that supports and rewards innovation, and provides the resources and infrastructure needed to pursue new ideas.

Celebrate success: Celebrate your successes, no matter how small. Recognizing and celebrating your achievements will help to build momentum and motivate you to continue innovating.

Embrace constraints: Constraints can be a powerful driver of innovation. Instead of viewing constraints as limitations, see them as opportunities to think creatively and find new solutions.

Be persistent: Innovation often requires persistence and perseverance. Don't give up on your ideas, even in the face of setbacks and obstacles.

Stay humble: Innovation requires a humble approach. Recognize that you don't have all the answers and be open to learning from others.

Seek out mentors who can provide guidance, support, and feedback on your ideas and approach.

Network: Networking can help you to connect with others who share your interests and can provide new insights and perspectives.

Develop a growth plan: Develop a plan for personal and professional growth that includes specific goals, timelines, and measurable outcomes. This will help you to stay focused and motivated on your innovation goals.

Use technology: Technology can be a powerful tool for innovation. Explore new technologies and use them to enhance your creativity and problem-solving skills.

Stay focused on the big picture: Innovation requires a long-term perspective. Stay focused on your vision and goals, and don't get bogged down by short-term setbacks or distractions.

Develop a sense of urgency: Innovation requires a sense of urgency and a willingness to take action. Develop a sense of urgency and prioritize your innovation efforts accordingly.

By incorporating these strategies into your mindset and approach to innovation, you can develop the skills and qualities needed to drive innovation and achieve success in your personal and professional life.

A **growth mindset** refers to the belief that one's abilities and intelligence can be developed over time through hard work, perseverance, and learning from mistakes. This mindset is in contrast to a fixed mindset, which is the belief that one's abilities and intelligence are fixed traits that cannot be changed.

Research shows that a growth mindset is essential for learning and achievement. People with a growth mindset tend to be more resilient in the face of challenges, more likely to persist in the face of difficulty, and more willing to take risks and try new things. They also tend to be more open to feedback and more likely to learn from their mistakes.

To develop a lifelong learning mindset, here are some strategies:

Embrace challenges: Seek out new challenges and opportunities to learn. Embrace the idea that challenges are opportunities for growth and learning.

Emphasize effort: Focus on the effort you put into learning, rather than just the outcome. Recognize that learning and growth require sustained effort and hard work.

Learn from mistakes: View mistakes as opportunities for learning and growth. Analyze what went wrong and how you can do better next time.

Seek out feedback: Be open to feedback from others, and use it to improve your performance. Recognize that feedback is an essential part of the learning process.

Cultivate curiosity: Develop a sense of curiosity and a desire to learn. Ask questions, explore new ideas, and seek out new information.

Practice self-reflection: Take time to reflect on your learning and growth. Reflect on what you have learned, what you still need to learn, and how you can continue to improve.

Surround yourself with learners: Surround yourself with people who value learning and growth. Seek out mentors, coaches, and peers who can support and challenge you in your learning journey.

Set goals: Set specific, measurable, and achievable goals for your learning. This will help you to stay focused and motivated, and to track your progress over time.

Use multiple learning modalities: Experiment with different learning modalities, such as reading, listening, watching videos, and hands-on practice. This will help you to engage with the material in different ways and to reinforce your learning.

Develop a growth mindset community: Connect with others who share your passion for learning and growth. This could be through online communities, local meetups, or professional organizations.

Be adaptable: Recognize that the world is constantly changing, and that learning is a lifelong process. Be willing to adapt and learn new skills as the world around you changes.

Take breaks: Finally, remember that learning is hard work, and that it's important to take breaks and give yourself time to rest and recharge. This will help you to maintain your energy and focus over the long term.

Practice mindfulness: Practicing mindfulness can help you to stay present and focused, which is essential for effective learning. Mindfulness practices such as meditation, deep breathing, and body scan exercises can help you to reduce stress, improve focus, and enhance your ability to learn.

Find inspiration: Seek out sources of inspiration that motivate you to learn and grow. This could be through reading books, watching TED talks, listening to podcasts, or attending conferences and workshops.

Embrace diversity: Be open to diverse perspectives and

experiences. Seek out opportunities to learn from people who are different from you, and be willing to question your own assumptions and biases.

Experiment with new approaches: Be willing to experiment with new approaches to learning and problem-solving. This could be through trying new study techniques, seeking out new mentors, or exploring new fields of study.

Practice reflection: Regularly reflect on your learning journey, and take time to celebrate your successes. Reflection can help you to identify areas where you have grown and to recognize the progress you have made.

Stay curious: Cultivate a sense of curiosity and wonder about the world around you. This can help you to stay engaged and motivated in your learning, and to continue exploring new ideas and topics.

Emphasize practical application: Look for ways to apply what you are learning in real-life situations. This can help you to solidify your understanding of the material, and to see the practical value of what you are learning.

Collaborate with others: Seek out opportunities to collaborate with others in your learning journey. This could be through study groups, online forums, or peer mentoring. Collaborating with others can help you to learn from different perspectives, and to support each other in achieving your goals.

Take ownership of your learning: Take responsibility for your own learning journey, and don't rely solely on teachers or mentors to guide you. Seek out opportunities to learn independently, and develop your own learning goals and strategies.

Focus on mastery: Instead of focusing on grades or test scores, focus on mastering the material and developing a deep understanding of the subject. This can help you to build a strong foundation of knowledge that will serve you well in the long term.

Be persistent: Learning can be challenging and frustrating at times, but it's important to stay persistent and keep working towards your goals. Remember that setbacks and failures are a natural part of the learning process, and that persistence and perseverance are key to success.

Celebrate progress: Finally, take time to celebrate your progress and accomplishments along the way. Recognize the hard work and effort that you have put into your learning, and celebrate the small victories that lead to bigger successes.

By incorporating these strategies into your daily life, you can develop a lifelong learning mindset that will help you to achieve your goals and find fulfillment in your personal and professional development. Remember that learning is a continuous process, and that by staying committed to growth and development, you can continue to learn and evolve throughout your life.

Mindset and **resilience** are closely related concepts that are both important for success in various areas of life.

Mindset refers to the collection of beliefs and attitudes that shape a person's outlook and approach to challenges and opportunities. A growth mindset, for example, is characterized by a belief that abilities can be developed through hard work and dedication, while a fixed mindset assumes that abilities are largely predetermined and unchangeable.

Resilience, on the other hand, refers to the ability to bounce back from setbacks, adapt to change, and persevere in the face of adversity. It is a key trait that can help individuals overcome obstacles, achieve their goals, and thrive in challenging environments.

The importance of resilience for success cannot be overstated. Life is full of unexpected challenges and setbacks, and those who are able to navigate these obstacles with resilience are more likely to achieve their goals and find fulfillment in their pursuits. Resilience also helps individuals to develop a sense of self-efficacy, or the belief in their ability to overcome challenges and achieve success.

Here are some strategies for developing resilience:

Cultivate a growth mindset: As mentioned earlier, a growth mindset is characterized by a belief in the ability to learn and grow through effort and experience. This mindset can help individuals view challenges as opportunities for growth and development, rather than insurmountable obstacles.

Build a support network: Having a strong support network of friends, family, and colleagues can provide emotional support and practical assistance during difficult times. It is important to cultivate these relationships and reach out for help when needed.

Practice self-care: Taking care of oneself is essential for building resilience. This includes getting enough sleep, eating a healthy diet, engaging in regular physical activity, and practicing stress-reduction techniques such as meditation or mindfulness.

Set realistic goals: Setting realistic goals that are achievable with effort can help build a sense of accomplishment and confidence. It is important to break larger goals into smaller, more manageable steps to avoid feeling overwhelmed.

Learn from setbacks: Rather than viewing setbacks as failures, it is important to view them as opportunities for growth and learning. Analyzing what went wrong and what can be done differently in the future can help build resilience and prevent future setbacks.

Develop problem-solving skills: Learning how to identify and solve problems can help build resilience. This involves breaking down complex issues into smaller, more manageable parts and developing strategies for addressing each component.

Practice positive thinking: Maintaining a positive outlook can help build resilience by fostering a sense of optimism and hope. This involves focusing on strengths and successes, rather than dwelling on failures and shortcomings.

Embrace challenges: Rather than avoiding challenges, it is important to embrace them as opportunities for growth and development. This may involve taking on new responsibilities, learning new skills, or stepping outside of one's comfort zone.

Practice flexibility: Being able to adapt to changing circumstances is essential for building resilience. This may involve being open to new ideas, adjusting one's expectations, or finding creative solutions to unexpected problems.

Seek professional help when needed: In some cases, building resilience may require working with a mental health professional or seeking support from a support group. It is important to recognize when additional help is needed and to seek it out without hesitation.

Practice gratitude: Regularly expressing gratitude for the good things in life, no matter how small, can help cultivate a positive outlook and build resilience. This involves focusing on what is going well, rather than dwelling on what is going wrong.

Develop healthy coping mechanisms: Everyone experiences stress and difficult emotions at some point in their lives, but it is important to develop healthy coping mechanisms for dealing with these feelings. This may involve engaging in relaxing activities like reading, listening to music, or spending time in nature, or seeking support from friends or a mental health professional.

Build emotional intelligence: Emotional intelligence involves the ability to recognize and regulate one's own emotions, as well as the emotions of others. Developing emotional intelligence can help build resilience by improving communication skills, increasing empathy, and reducing stress and anxiety.

Practice mindfulness: Mindfulness involves being fully present in the moment and focusing on one's thoughts, feelings, and sensations without judgment. Practicing mindfulness can help build resilience by reducing stress, improving focus and concentration, and increasing awareness of one's own thoughts and emotions.

Learn from role models: Observing and learning from the experiences of others who have demonstrated resilience can be a powerful way to build one's own resilience. This may involve seeking out mentors or reading biographies of individuals who have overcome adversity.

Practice self-compassion: Treating oneself with kindness and compassion can help build resilience by reducing self- criticism and negative self-talk. This involves acknowledging and accepting one's own shortcomings and mistakes, rather than beating oneself up over them.

Keep a growth mindset journal: Keeping a journal to reflect on one's experiences and progress can help cultivate a growth mindset and build resilience. This involves recording successes and setbacks, identifying areas for improvement, and setting goals for the future.

Stay connected to one's values: Staying connected to one's core values and beliefs can provide a sense of purpose and direction, even during difficult times. This involves reflecting on what is most important in life and making decisions that align with those values.

Take action: Taking action, no matter how small, can help build resilience by creating a sense of momentum and progress. This involves identifying concrete steps that can be taken to move toward one's goals, and then taking those steps consistently over time.

Celebrate progress: Celebrating progress, no matter how small, can help build resilience by fostering a sense of accomplishment and motivation. This involves acknowledging and celebrating successes along the way, rather than waiting for a final outcome.

Developing resilience takes time and effort, but it is a skill that can be learned and strengthened over time. By incorporating these strategies into their daily lives, individuals can build the resilience needed to overcome challenges and achieve their goals. It is important to remember that resilience is not about being invincible or never experiencing setbacks, but rather about developing the ability to bounce back from adversity and continue moving forward.

Mindset and **confidence** are closely related. Our mindset refers to our attitudes, beliefs, and thoughts about ourselves and the world around us. Our confidence, on the other hand, is our belief in our abilities and our trust in ourselves to achieve our goals. A positive mindset can lead to greater confidence, while a negative mindset can lead to low confidence and self-doubt.

Here are some strategies for building confidence:

Identify and challenge negative self-talk: Pay attention to the negative thoughts you have about yourself and replace them with positive ones. For example, if you catch yourself thinking "I'm not good enough," replace it with "I am capable of achieving my goals."

Set achievable goals: Break down your larger goals into smaller, achievable steps. This will help you build confidence as you see yourself making progress towards your goals.

Celebrate successes: When you achieve a goal, take the time to acknowledge and celebrate your success. This will help reinforce your confidence and motivate you to continue working towards your goals.

Practice self-care: Taking care of yourself physically, emotionally, and mentally can help boost your confidence. This includes getting enough rest, eating healthy, exercising, and engaging in activities that bring you joy.

Surround yourself with positive people: Spend time with people who uplift and support you. This can help you build a positive mindset and reinforce your confidence.

Learn and improve: Take opportunities to learn new skills or improve upon existing ones. This can help you build confidence in your abilities and increase your overall self-efficacy.

Remember, building confidence takes time and effort. Be patient with yourself and keep working towards your goals.

Visualize success: Imagine yourself achieving your goals and visualize the steps you need to take to get there. This can help you build confidence and motivate you to take action towards your goals.

Take risks: Stepping outside of your comfort zone and taking on new challenges can help you build confidence. Even if you don't succeed, you will have learned from the experience and gained valuable knowledge and skills.

Practice gratitude: Take the time to appreciate the things you have in your life and the progress you have made towards your goals. This can help you build a positive mindset and increase your overall sense of well-being.

Focus on solutions: When faced with challenges, focus on finding solutions rather than dwelling on the problem. This can help you build confidence in your problem-solving abilities.

Embrace failure: Failure is a natural part of the learning process. Instead of letting failure hold you back, use it as an opportunity to learn and grow. This can help you build resilience and increase your overall confidence.

Seek feedback: Ask for feedback from others and be open to constructive criticism. This can help you identify areas for improvement and build confidence in your abilities.

Practice mindfulness: Mindfulness is the practice of being present and fully engaged in the current moment. Practicing mindfulness can help you build a positive mindset and reduce feelings of stress and anxiety, which can often undermine confidence.

Use positive affirmations: Positive affirmations are statements that you repeat to yourself to reinforce positive beliefs and attitudes. For example, you might say, "I am capable and confident" or "I trust in my abilities to achieve my goals."

Keep a success journal: Write down your successes and accomplishments in a journal or notebook. This can help you reflect on your progress and build confidence in your abilities.

Take care of your appearance: Taking care of your physical appearance can help you feel more confident and self- assured. This includes things like dressing well, grooming, and maintaining good posture.

Practice assertiveness: Assertiveness is the ability to express your needs and opinions in a clear and confident manner. Practicing assertiveness can help you build confidence and improve your communication skills.

Volunteer or help others: Helping others can boost your self-esteem and give you a sense of purpose and accomplishment. This can help you build confidence and develop a positive mindset.

Remember, building confidence is a process that requires patience and persistence. It's important to stay committed to your goals and to keep working on building a positive mindset and reinforcing your beliefs in your abilities. With time and effort, you can develop the confidence you need to succeed in all areas of your life.

Mindset and **persistence** are closely related because one's mindset can greatly influence their ability to persevere in the face of obstacles and challenges. A growth mindset, which is the belief that skills and abilities can be developed through dedication and hard work, is associated with greater persistence than a fixed mindset, which is the belief that skills and abilities are innate and cannot be changed.

The role of mindset in persistence can be seen in how people respond to failure. Those with a growth mindset are more likely to view failure as an opportunity to learn and improve, while those with a fixed mindset may be more likely to give up after experiencing failure.

Strategies for developing persistence include:

Setting goals: Having clear and specific goals can provide motivation and direction for working towards a desired outcome.

Breaking tasks into manageable steps: Large tasks can feel overwhelming, but breaking them down into smaller, more manageable steps can make them feel less daunting.

Building a support system: Surrounding oneself with supportive people who can offer encouragement and guidance can help maintain motivation and perseverance.

Embracing failure: Seeing failure as a natural part of the learning process can help individuals maintain a growth mindset and continue to work towards their goals.

Celebrating successes: Recognizing and celebrating small successes along the way can provide a sense of accomplishment and help maintain motivation.

Developing a positive attitude: Maintaining a positive attitude, even in the face of challenges, can help individuals maintain their motivation and focus on the task at hand.

Practicing mindfulness: Mindfulness techniques, such as

meditation or deep breathing, can help individuals stay focused and calm during challenging situations.

Seeking feedback: Asking for feedback from others can help individuals identify areas for improvement and make adjustments as needed.

Learning from others: Studying the strategies and approaches of successful individuals can provide inspiration and guidance for developing persistence and achieving goals.

Cultivating a growth mindset: As mentioned earlier, a growth mindset is associated with greater persistence. One way to cultivate a growth mindset is to embrace challenges and view them as opportunities for growth and learning.

Visualizing success: Visualization techniques can help individuals maintain motivation and focus by creating a mental picture of their desired outcome.

Keeping a positive self-talk: The way we talk to ourselves can greatly impact our level of persistence. Practicing positive self-talk can help individuals stay motivated and focused on their goals.

Taking calculated risks: Taking calculated risks can help individuals push themselves out of their comfort zone and develop resilience in the face of challenges.

Learning from failures: Analyzing failures can help individuals identify areas for improvement and adjust their approach accordingly. This can help build resilience and persistence over time.

Creating a plan: Having a clear and actionable plan can help individuals stay organized and focused on their goals. Breaking down the plan into specific tasks and deadlines can also help create a sense of urgency and motivation.

Tracking progress: Regularly tracking progress towards a goal can help individuals stay motivated and identify areas where they may need to adjust their approach.

Using positive affirmations: Practicing positive affirmations can help individuals maintain a positive mindset and stay motivated during challenging times.

Seeking support from a mentor or coach: Working with a mentor or coach can provide guidance, encouragement, and accountability, all of which can help individuals develop persistence and achieve their goals.

Embracing discomfort: Growth and learning often require stepping outside of one's comfort zone, which can be uncomfortable. Embracing discomfort and pushing past it can help individuals build resilience and persistence over time.

Staying flexible: Being able to adapt to changing circumstances and adjust one's approach as needed can help individuals maintain momentum and persevere through challenges.

Developing persistence is not always easy, but with the right mindset, strategies, and practices, individuals can build the resilience they need to achieve their goals and succeed in the face of challenges.

Having a **growth mindset** can be extremely beneficial for developing laser-like focus. A growth mindset is the belief that your abilities and intelligence can be developed through hard work and dedication. This mindset allows you to approach challenges with a positive attitude and a willingness to learn and improve, which can help you stay focused on your goals.

Here are some strategies for developing laser-like focus:

Set clear goals: Having clear and specific goals can help you stay focused and motivated. Write down your goals and break them down into smaller, more manageable tasks.

Eliminate distractions: Identify the things that distract you and try to eliminate them as much as possible. This could mean turning off your phone, closing your email inbox, or finding a quiet workspace.

Practice mindfulness: Mindfulness is the practice of being present and fully engaged in the current moment. This can help you stay focused and avoid getting sidetracked by negative thoughts or distractions.

Take breaks: Taking short breaks can actually help improve your focus and productivity. Try taking a 5-10 minute break every hour to rest your mind and recharge.

Focus on one task at a time: Multitasking can actually reduce productivity and increase stress. Instead, focus on one task at a time and give it your full attention.

Embrace challenges: Embrace challenges as opportunities to learn and grow, rather than viewing them as obstacles. This can help you stay motivated and focused on achieving your goals.

By adopting a growth mindset and implementing these strategies, you can develop laser-like focus and achieve your goals more effectively.

Use positive self-talk: Your inner dialogue can have a big impact on your ability to focus. Use positive self-talk to encourage and motivate yourself, especially in moments of difficulty or distraction.

Prioritize your tasks: Prioritize your tasks based on their importance and urgency. This can help you stay focused on the tasks that matter most and avoid getting sidetracked by less important tasks.

Use a timer: Set a timer for a specific amount of time, such as 25 minutes, and work on a task without interruption until the timer goes off. This technique, known as the Pomodoro Technique, can help you stay focused and avoid distractions.

Get enough sleep: Lack of sleep can negatively impact your ability to focus and be productive. Make sure you're getting enough sleep each night to help you stay focused and engaged throughout the day.

Practice visualization: Visualization is the practice of creating a mental picture of yourself successfully completing a task or achieving a goal. This can help you stay motivated and focused on your goals.

Take care of yourself: Eating a balanced diet, exercising regularly, and practicing self-care can all help improve your focus and productivity. Make sure you're taking care of yourself both physically and mentally to help you stay focused and energized.

Create a conducive environment: Your environment can have a big impact on your ability to focus. Create a workspace that is comfortable, well-lit, and free from distractions. You can also try using noise-cancelling headphones or playing background music to help you stay focused.

Break down big tasks: Big tasks can be overwhelming and can make it difficult to stay focused. Break down big tasks into smaller, more manageable tasks to make them less daunting. This can help you stay focused and motivated as you work through each task.

Practice active listening: Active listening is the practice of fully engaging with and understanding what someone is saying. This can help you stay focused during meetings or conversations and avoid getting distracted.

Take care of your mental health: Stress, anxiety, and other mental health issues can make it difficult to stay focused. Take care of your mental health by practicing self-care, seeking support from friends or a mental health professional, and taking breaks when you need them.

Learn to say no: Saying yes to too many commitments or tasks can make it difficult to stay focused on your priorities. Learn to say no to things that don't align with your goals or values, and prioritize your time and energy accordingly.

Celebrate small wins: Celebrating small accomplishments along the way can help you stay motivated and focused on your goals. Take time to acknowledge and celebrate your progress as you work toward your larger goals.

Stay organized: Staying organized can help you stay focused and avoid getting overwhelmed. Keep a to-do list, use a planner, or try a project management tool to help you stay on track with your tasks and goals.

Take care of your physical health: Your physical health can have a big impact on your ability to focus. Make sure you're eating a healthy diet, staying hydrated, and getting regular exercise to help you stay focused and energized.

Find a accountability partner: Having someone to hold you accountable can help you stay focused and motivated. Find a friend, family member, or colleague who can support you and hold you accountable as you work toward your goals.

Use positive affirmations: Positive affirmations are statements that promote positive self-talk and self-belief. Use positive affirmations to help you stay focused and motivated, especially when you're feeling discouraged or distracted.

Practice deep breathing: Deep breathing can help you relax, reduce stress, and improve your focus. Take a few deep breaths whenever you're feeling stressed or distracted to help you refocus and re-energize.

Take care of your eyesight: If you spend a lot of time looking at screens, it's important to take care of your eyesight. Take breaks to look away from your screen, adjust your screen's brightness and contrast, and make sure you're sitting at a comfortable distance from your screen.

By implementing these strategies and developing a growth mindset, you can improve your focus and achieve your goals more effectively. Remember that developing laser-like focus takes time and practice, so be patient with yourself and keep working toward your goals.

Mindset and **motivation** are closely related. Mindset refers to the beliefs and attitudes that individuals hold about themselves, their abilities, and the world around them. Motivation, on the other hand, refers to the internal or external factors that drive individuals to take action towards a particular goal.

Research has shown that individuals' mindset can significantly impact their motivation levels. Individuals with a growth mindset, for example, tend to be more motivated because they believe that they can improve their abilities through effort and practice. In contrast, individuals with a fixed mindset may be less motivated because they believe that their abilities are fixed and cannot be improved.

Strategies for boosting motivation include:

Setting clear and specific goals: Having clear and specific goals helps individuals to focus their attention and efforts towards achieving them.

Creating a plan of action: Breaking down goals into smaller, manageable steps can help individuals to stay motivated by providing a sense of progress and accomplishment.

Building a support system: Surrounding oneself with supportive and encouraging people can provide individuals with the necessary motivation and accountability to achieve their goals.

Celebrating small wins: Celebrating small victories along the way can help individuals to stay motivated by reinforcing their progress and providing a sense of accomplishment.

Practicing positive self-talk: Positive self-talk can help individuals to maintain a positive mindset and stay motivated even when faced with challenges or setbacks.

Rewarding oneself: Offering oneself small rewards for achieving certain milestones can help to maintain motivation and provide an extra incentive to continue working towards one's goals.

Focusing on intrinsic motivation: Individuals who are motivated by internal factors, such as personal fulfillment or a sense of purpose, are more likely to maintain their motivation over the long term.

Identifying obstacles and developing strategies to overcome them: When individuals identify potential obstacles that may hinder their progress towards their goals, they can develop strategies to overcome them, which can help to maintain motivation.

Finding meaning in the task: When individuals find meaning in the task or goal they are working towards, it can help to increase motivation levels. For example, if someone is studying for an exam, they may find meaning in the fact that passing the exam will help them achieve their career goals.

Practicing mindfulness: Mindfulness practices, such as meditation or deep breathing, can help individuals to reduce stress and anxiety, which can often be a barrier to motivation.

Setting a schedule: Creating a schedule or routine can help individuals to stay on track and maintain motivation by providing structure and a sense of control.

Visualizing success: Visualizing oneself achieving the desired outcome can help individuals to stay motivated by providing a clear mental image of what they are working towards.

Tracking progress: Keeping track of progress towards a goal can help individuals to stay motivated by providing a sense of accomplishment and highlighting areas where improvement is needed.

Remember, everyone's motivation is unique, and what works for one person may not work for another. It's important to experiment with different strategies and find what works best for you.

Emphasizing the benefits of taking action: Focusing on the positive outcomes that can result from taking action towards a goal can help individuals to stay motivated. For example, if someone is trying to lose weight, they may focus on the health benefits of exercise and healthy eating.

Making the task enjoyable: Finding ways to make the task or goal more enjoyable can help individuals to stay motivated. For example, if someone is trying to learn a new language, they may watch movies or TV shows in that language to make it more enjoyable.

Using positive reinforcement: Using positive reinforcement, such as rewards or praise, can help individuals to stay motivated by reinforcing positive behaviors.

Finding accountability partners: Having someone to hold you accountable can help to maintain motivation. This could be a friend, family member, or a coach who checks in regularly on your progress.

Breaking the task into smaller, more manageable pieces: Breaking a large task into smaller, more manageable pieces can help individuals to stay motivated by providing a sense of progress and accomplishment.

Reflecting on past successes: Reflecting on past successes can help individuals to stay motivated by reminding them of their past accomplishments and reinforcing their abilities.

Seeking inspiration: Finding inspiration from others who have achieved similar goals can help individuals to stay motivated. This could involve reading success stories or watching motivational videos.

Practicing self-care: Taking care of oneself, both physically and mentally, can help individuals to maintain motivation. This could involve getting enough sleep, eating well, and engaging in activities that bring joy and relaxation.

Recognizing and addressing negative self-talk: Negative self-talk can be a barrier to motivation. Recognizing and addressing negative thoughts can help individuals to maintain a positive mindset and stay motivated.

Embracing failure as a part of the learning process: Failure is a natural part of the learning process. Embracing failure and using it as an opportunity to learn and grow can help individuals to maintain motivation and continue working towards their goals.

Finding a sense of purpose: Having a sense of purpose can help individuals to stay motivated by providing a clear reason for why they are working towards their goals.

Using technology to stay on track: There are many tools and apps available that can help individuals to stay on track and maintain motivation. For example, a habit-tracking app can help individuals to build positive habits over time.

Embracing a growth mindset: Embracing a growth mindset, which involves believing that abilities can be developed through effort and practice, can help individuals to maintain motivation and continue working towards their goals.

Remember, boosting motivation is a process that requires effort and persistence. By incorporating some of these strategies into your routine, you can increase your motivation levels and achieve your goals.

Mindset plays a crucial role in **decision-making** because it shapes the way individuals approach challenges, process information, and evaluate potential outcomes. Individuals with a growth mindset tend to view challenges as opportunities for learning and growth, while those with a fixed mindset may view challenges as threats to their abilities and potential. Consequently, people with a growth mindset are more likely to take risks, embrace new experiences, and persist through difficult situations, all of which are important qualities for effective decision- making.

Here are some strategies for developing a growth mindset for decision-making:

Embrace challenges: Instead of avoiding difficult decisions or situations, try to embrace them as opportunities for growth and learning. Reframe your mindset to see challenges as chances to develop new skills and expand your knowledge.

Learn from failure: Instead of viewing failure as a personal shortcoming, try to see it as a natural part of the learning process. Analyze what went wrong and use that knowledge to inform future decisions.

Seek out feedback: Feedback is essential for growth and development. Seek out constructive criticism from others and use it to improve your decision-making abilities.

Cultivate curiosity: Approach decision-making with an open and curious mind. Ask questions, seek out new perspectives, and challenge your assumptions.

Practice mindfulness: Mindfulness can help you become more aware of your thoughts and emotions, which can help you make better decisions. Take time to reflect on your decision-making process, and use mindfulness techniques like deep breathing or meditation to stay focused and centered.

Focus on the process, not just the outcome: Instead of solely focusing on the end result, pay attention to the steps you take to get there. This can help you identify areas for improvement and adjust your decision-making process accordingly.

Take calculated risks: While it's important to take risks in order to grow, it's also important to be strategic about it. Take calculated risks by weighing the potential benefits and drawbacks of each option before making a decision.

Emphasize learning over success: Instead of only valuing success, place a greater emphasis on the learning process. This can help you view setbacks as opportunities for growth and development.

Surround yourself with growth-minded individuals: The people we surround ourselves with can have a big impact on our mindset. Seek out peers, mentors, or colleagues who have a growth mindset and can offer support and encouragement.

Practice self-compassion: Be kind to yourself and acknowledge that mistakes and failures are a natural part of the learning process. Practice self-compassion by treating yourself with the same kindness and understanding you would offer to a friend.

Embrace challenges outside of your comfort zone: By stepping outside of your comfort zone, you can expose yourself to new experiences and opportunities for growth. Challenge yourself to take on tasks or make decisions that you wouldn't normally consider.

Celebrate progress: Instead of solely focusing on the end goal, take time to celebrate the progress you've made along the way. Recognize the small victories and milestones you achieve as you work towards your larger goals.

By incorporating these strategies into your decision-making process, you can develop a growth mindset that allows you to approach challenges with greater confidence and resilience. Remember that developing a growth mindset is an ongoing process, and it takes time and effort to cultivate a mindset that is focused on learning and growth.

A growth mindset is a key component of **effective time management.** Having a growth mindset means that you believe that your abilities and skills can be developed through dedication and hard work. This mindset empowers you to take charge of your time and use it wisely to achieve your goals.

Here are some strategies for developing effective time management skills with a growth mindset:

Set clear goals: Setting clear goals is essential for effective time management. Define what you want to achieve and break it down into smaller, manageable tasks. This will help you stay focused and motivated.

Prioritize tasks: Prioritize your tasks based on their importance and urgency. This will help you focus on the most important tasks and avoid wasting time on less important ones.

Use a schedule: Use a schedule or planner to organize your time. This will help you stay on track and ensure that you have enough time for all your tasks and activities.

Avoid multitasking: Multitasking can actually be counterproductive. Instead of trying to do multiple tasks at once, focus on one task at a time and give it your full attention.

Learn to say no: Learning to say no to unnecessary tasks and activities can help you free up time for more important things.

Practice self-discipline: Self-discipline is key to effective time management. Avoid procrastination and stay focused on your goals.

Learn from your mistakes: Don't be afraid to make mistakes. Learn from them and use them as opportunities to improve your time management skills.

Take breaks: Taking breaks is important for maintaining focus and productivity. Make sure to schedule regular breaks throughout your day to recharge your batteries.

Manage distractions: Distractions can be a major time-waster. Identify your biggest distractions and find ways to manage or eliminate them. For example, you might turn off your phone during work hours or use website blockers to avoid getting sidetracked by social media.

Track your time: Keep track of how you're spending your time. This will help you identify areas where you're wasting time and make adjustments to your schedule as needed.

Delegate tasks: Delegating tasks to others can help you free up time for more important activities. Identify tasks that can be delegated and find someone who can help you with them.

Stay flexible: Even with the best time management strategies in place, unexpected events can still disrupt your schedule. Stay flexible and be prepared to adjust your plans when necessary.

Celebrate your successes: Celebrate your successes, no matter how small. This will help you stay motivated and maintain a positive attitude towards your work.

Eliminate unnecessary tasks: Take a critical look at your to-do list and identify tasks that are not essential. Eliminating unnecessary tasks can help you streamline your schedule and free up more time for important activities.

Take care of yourself: Taking care of yourself is essential for effective time management. Make sure to get enough sleep, eat well, and exercise regularly. When you're feeling good physically and mentally, you'll be better equipped to manage your time effectively.

Find a mentor: Finding a mentor who has strong time management skills can be incredibly helpful. They can provide guidance and support as you work to develop your own time management skills.

Learn to say yes: While it's important to learn to say no to unnecessary tasks, it's also important to learn to say yes to opportunities that align with your goals. Taking on new challenges can help you grow and develop your skills.

Reflect on your progress: Take time to reflect on your progress and identify areas where you can improve. Celebrate your successes and use your failures as learning opportunities.

Keep learning: Keep learning and growing your skills. Attend training courses, read books, and seek out new experiences that can help you develop your time management skills.

Break tasks into smaller chunks: Breaking tasks into smaller, more manageable chunks can help you avoid feeling overwhelmed and make it easier to stay focused and motivated.

Use the Pomodoro technique: The Pomodoro technique involves breaking your workday into 25-minute intervals (known as "Pomodoros") with short breaks in between. This can help you stay focused and productive throughout the day.

Ask for help: Don't be afraid to ask for help when you need it. Whether it's delegating tasks to others or asking for advice from a mentor, reaching out for support can help you manage your time more effectively.

Stay organized: Staying organized is essential for effective time management. Keep your workspace clean and tidy, use a filing system to organize your documents, and make sure to keep your schedule and to-do list up to date.

Focus on your strengths: Identify your strengths and focus on activities that allow you to use them. When you're doing work that aligns with your strengths, you'll be more engaged and motivated, which can help you manage your time more effectively.

Learn from others: Take inspiration from others who have strong time management skills. Whether it's a colleague at work or a public figure you admire, observing how others manage their time can help you develop your own skills.

Remember that effective time management requires consistent effort and practice. By adopting a growth mindset and implementing these strategies, you can become a master of your time and achieve your goals more efficiently.

Mindset and **gratitude** are closely related. A growth mindset is the belief that abilities and intelligence can be developed through hard work and dedication, while a fixed mindset is the belief that intelligence and abilities are static and cannot be changed. Practicing gratitude is a powerful way to cultivate a growth mindset, as it helps individuals focus on the positive aspects of their lives and appreciate the progress they have made.

The benefits of practicing gratitude are numerous. Gratitude has been linked to increased happiness, improved relationships, better physical health, and increased resilience. People who regularly practice gratitude also tend to be more optimistic and have a more positive outlook on life.

There are several strategies for cultivating gratitude, including:

Keeping a gratitude journal: Write down three things you are grateful for each day. This can help you focus on the positive aspects of your life and appreciate the good things that happen to you.

Expressing gratitude to others: Take time to thank the people in your life who have helped you or made a positive impact on you. This can help strengthen your relationships and improve your overall sense of well-being.

Practicing mindfulness: Take a few minutes each day to focus on the present moment and appreciate the world around you. This can help you develop a deeper sense of gratitude and appreciation for the simple things in life.

Reframing negative experiences: Try to find the silver lining in difficult situations. This can help you develop a more positive outlook and cultivate gratitude even in challenging times.

Increased happiness: Gratitude can help boost feelings of happiness and contentment. When you focus on the positive aspects of your life, you are more likely to feel happy and satisfied with what you have.

Improved relationships: Expressing gratitude to others can help strengthen your relationships and improve your connections with others. When you take the time to thank others for their contributions, you are more likely to feel connected and appreciated.

Better physical health: Gratitude has been linked to improved physical health, including better sleep, reduced stress, and lower levels of inflammation.

Increased resilience: Practicing gratitude can help you develop a more resilient mindset. When you focus on the positive aspects of your life, you are better able to cope with challenges and setbacks.

Improved self-esteem: Gratitude can help boost feelings of self-worth and self-esteem. When you appreciate the good things in your life, you are more likely to feel good about yourself and your abilities.

Reflect on the good things in your life: Take some time each day to reflect on the things you are grateful for. This can be as simple as taking a few minutes to think about the good things that happened to you that day.

Practice gratitude with a partner: If you have a partner, take some time each day to share the things you are grateful for with each other. This can help strengthen your relationship and increase feelings of connection and appreciation.

Volunteer or give back: Helping others can be a powerful way to cultivate gratitude and appreciation for what you have. Consider volunteering at a local organization or donating to a charity that resonates with you.

Use visual reminders: Place reminders of the things you are grateful for in visible places around your home or office. This could be a photo of a loved one, a note of appreciation, or a piece of artwork that reminds you of something positive.

Engage in acts of kindness: Doing something kind for someone else can be a powerful way to cultivate gratitude and appreciation for the good in your life. Consider doing something kind for a stranger or friend, such as offering a compliment or buying them a small gift.

Remember, cultivating gratitude is a practice that takes time and effort. By incorporating these strategies into your daily routine, you can develop a more positive mindset and improve your overall well-being.

Mindset is a term used to describe a person's underlying attitudes, beliefs, and assumptions about themselves and their abilities. It can be influenced by a variety of factors, including past experiences, cultural and social norms, and personal values. One important factor that can impact mindset is self-talk.

Self-talk refers to the internal dialogue that a person has with themselves. It can be positive or negative and can have a profound impact on a person's mindset. Negative self-talk can lead to self-doubt, anxiety, and a lack of confidence, while positive self-talk can help promote self-confidence, resilience, and a growth mindset.

Pay attention to your self-talk: The first step in developing positive self-talk is to become aware of your current self- talk patterns. Pay attention to the thoughts that run through your mind and try to identify any negative or self- limiting beliefs.

Challenge negative self-talk: Once you have identified negative self-talk patterns, challenge them by questioning their validity. Ask yourself if there is any evidence to support these negative thoughts. Often, negative self-talk is based on fear or insecurity rather than reality.

Use positive affirmations: Affirmations are positive statements that can help reprogram your mind to think positively. Create a list of affirmations that reflect your goals and values, and repeat them to yourself regularly.

Focus on solutions: When faced with a challenge or obstacle, focus on finding a solution rather than dwelling on the problem. Use positive self-talk to encourage yourself to take action and overcome the challenge.

Practice self-compassion: Treat yourself with kindness and understanding, even when you make mistakes. Use positive self-talk to remind yourself that everyone makes mistakes and that failure is an opportunity to learn and grow.

Use visualization: Visualization is a powerful tool for building confidence and optimism. Picture yourself achieving your goals, and use positive self-talk to reinforce the vision. This can help you to stay motivated and focused on your goals.

Surround yourself with positivity: The people you spend time with can have a big impact on your mindset. Surround yourself with positive, supportive people who encourage and uplift you. This can help you to maintain a positive outlook and reinforce positive self-talk.

Celebrate your successes: When you achieve a goal or overcome a challenge, take time to celebrate your success. Use positive self-talk to acknowledge your hard work and accomplishments. This can help to build confidence and reinforce positive self-talk.

Reframe negative thoughts: Reframing negative thoughts is a technique that involves looking at a situation from a different perspective. Instead of focusing on the negative aspects of a situation, try to find the positive. For example, instead of saying "I can't do this," reframe it as "This is a challenge, but I'm going to find a way to overcome it."

Use humor: Humor can be a powerful tool for reducing stress and promoting positivity. Use lighthearted humor to diffuse negative self-talk and change your perspective. For example, if you make a mistake, instead of beating yourself up, make a joke about it and move on.

Practice gratitude: Gratitude is the practice of focusing on the positive things in your life and being thankful for them. Use positive self-talk to express gratitude for the good things in your life. This can help to shift your focus from negative self-talk to positive self-talk.

Learn from mistakes: Instead of seeing mistakes as failures, use them as learning opportunities. Use positive self- talk to acknowledge what you've learned from your mistakes and how you can use that knowledge to improve in the future.

Set realistic goals: Setting realistic goals can help to build confidence and promote positive self-talk. Use positive self-talk to encourage yourself to set achievable goals and celebrate your progress along the way.

Remember, developing positive self-talk is an ongoing process that requires practice and dedication. The more you practice positive self-talk, the more natural it will become, and the more positive your mindset will be. With persistence and a commitment to self-improvement, you can transform your mindset and achieve your goals with confidence and resilience.

Mindset refers to our beliefs and attitudes about ourselves and the world around us. Our mindset can influence how we approach challenges and setbacks, including failure. There are two main types of mindsets: a fixed mindset and a growth mindset.

A fixed mindset is the belief that our abilities and intelligence are fixed traits that cannot be changed. People with a fixed mindset may feel discouraged by failure because they interpret it as evidence of their inherent limitations.

A growth mindset, on the other hand, is the belief that our abilities and intelligence can be developed through hard work and persistence. People with a growth mindset see failure as an opportunity to learn and improve, rather than as a reflection of their limitations.

Developing a growth mindset can help us overcome failure by allowing us to view it as a natural part of the learning process. Here are some strategies for developing a growth mindset in the face of failure:

Embrace challenges: Seek out challenges that push you out of your comfort zone. Embracing challenges can help you develop resilience and overcome setbacks.

Focus on effort: Instead of focusing on the outcome, focus on the effort you put in. Recognize that effort is what leads to growth and improvement.

Learn from failure: Instead of dwelling on your mistakes, use them as an opportunity to learn and grow. Reflect on what went wrong, and how you can do better next time.

Practice self-compassion: Be kind and understanding with yourself when you experience failure. Recognize that failure is a natural part of the learning process, and that everyone experiences setbacks at some point.

Surround yourself with a growth mindset: Surround yourself with people who have a growth mindset. Their positive attitudes and perspectives can help you develop a more positive outlook on failure.

Challenge negative self-talk: When you experience failure, it's easy to fall into negative self-talk. Challenge those negative thoughts by asking yourself if they are really true, and if there is evidence to support them.

Set realistic goals: Set goals that are challenging, but also achievable. This can help you build confidence and momentum as you work towards your goals.

Seek feedback: Ask for feedback from others, and use it to improve your skills and knowledge. Be open to constructive criticism, and use it as an opportunity to learn and grow.

Focus on the process: Instead of focusing solely on the end result, focus on the process of learning and growing. Celebrate the small successes and progress you make along the way.

Cultivate curiosity: Approach failures and setbacks with a sense of curiosity and a desire to learn. Ask questions and seek out new information that can help you improve.

Take calculated risks: Be willing to take calculated risks and try new things, even if they might lead to failure. This can help you build resilience and develop new skills and knowledge.

Stay flexible: Be flexible and adaptable in the face of failure and setbacks. Remember that there are often multiple paths to success, and be willing to pivot and adjust your approach as needed.

Celebrate progress: Celebrate the progress you make, no matter how small. Recognize that every step towards your goal is a step in the right direction, and use that momentum to keep moving forward.

Find a mentor: Seek out a mentor who can provide guidance and support as you work towards your goals. A mentor can also help you develop new skills and knowledge, and provide valuable feedback on your progress.

Stay motivated: Stay motivated by focusing on your long-term goals, and by reminding yourself of why you started in the first place. Break down your goals into smaller, more manageable steps, and celebrate each milestone along the way.

Practice self-reflection: Take time to reflect on your experiences, and use those reflections to inform your future actions. This can help you identify areas for improvement, and develop new strategies for success.

Remember, developing a growth mindset is an ongoing process. It requires effort, persistence, and a willingness to learn and grow. But with practice, you can develop a growth mindset that allows you to overcome failure and achieve success in all areas of your life.

Part II

THE POWER OF PURPOSE

Purpose driven leadership is a leadership style that centers around a leader's commitment to a shared purpose or mission that goes beyond just earning profits or achieving short-term goals. A purpose driven leader is someone who is passionate about a cause or vision, and who inspires and motivates others to work towards that vision.

One of the key characteristics of purpose driven leadership is a focus on long-term goals and sustainability. Purpose driven leaders are often more concerned with creating lasting change and making a positive impact on society, rather than just achieving short-term gains.

Another important characteristic of purpose driven leadership is the ability to build strong relationships with stakeholders. Purpose driven leaders understand that their success is dependent on the success of their team, and they work to build trust and collaboration with their employees and other stakeholders.

Purpose driven leaders also tend to be strong communicators and storytellers. They are able to articulate their vision in a way that inspires and motivates others, and they are skilled at communicating their message in a way that resonates with people on an emotional level.

Finally, purpose driven leaders are often focused on continuous learning and personal growth. They understand that in order to lead effectively, they need to be constantly learning and adapting to new challenges and opportunities.

Authenticity: Purpose driven leaders are genuine and authentic in their communication and leadership style. They are transparent about their values, beliefs, and intentions, and they lead by example, modeling the behavior they expect from others.

Empathy: Purpose driven leaders are empathetic and understanding of the needs and perspectives of others. They listen actively to their team members, customers, and other stakeholders, and they are responsive to their concerns and feedback.

Flexibility: Purpose driven leaders are adaptable and flexible in their approach to leadership. They recognize that change is constant, and they are open to new ideas and perspectives.

Visionary: Purpose driven leaders are visionary and forward-thinking. They have a clear and compelling vision for the future, and they are able to inspire and motivate others to work towards that vision.

Collaborative: Purpose driven leaders are collaborative and inclusive in their leadership style. They recognize that achieving their purpose requires the input and support of others, and they work to build strong partnerships and collaborations with stakeholders.

Ethical: Purpose driven leaders are ethical and principled in their decision-making. They prioritize doing what is right and just, even if it means making difficult or unpopular decisions.

Resilient: Purpose driven leaders are resilient and persistent in the face of challenges and setbacks. They are able to stay focused on their purpose and vision, even in the face of obstacles and adversity.

Empowerment: Purpose driven leaders empower their team members by delegating responsibilities and providing them with the tools and resources they need to succeed. They trust their team members, encourage them to take ownership of their work, and provide them with opportunities for growth and development.

Continuous improvement: Purpose driven leaders are committed to continuous improvement. They are always seeking ways to enhance their skills and knowledge, and they encourage their team members to do the same. They are open to feedback and willing to make changes to improve their leadership style and achieve their purpose.

Accountability: Purpose driven leaders hold themselves and their team members accountable for their actions and results. They set clear expectations, provide feedback and coaching, and recognize and reward success. They also take responsibility for their mistakes and failures and use them as opportunities for growth and learning.

Social responsibility: Purpose driven leaders are committed to social responsibility and making a positive impact on society. They are aware of the broader social and environmental implications of their actions, and they work to ensure that their organizations are contributing to the greater good.

Creativity: Purpose driven leaders are creative and innovative in their approach to problem-solving and achieving their purpose. They are willing to take risks and try new things, and they encourage their team members to do the same. They also recognize the value of diversity and different perspectives in driving innovation and creativity.

Decisiveness: Purpose driven leaders are decisive and able to make tough decisions when necessary. They are able to balance competing priorities and make decisions that are aligned with their purpose and values.

Emotional intelligence: Purpose driven leaders possess high emotional intelligence and are able to understand and manage their own emotions and those of others. They are empathetic, able to read the emotions of others, and able to use this information to build stronger relationships and make better decisions.

Inclusivity: Purpose driven leaders are inclusive and value diversity. They recognize that a diverse team brings a range of perspectives and ideas, and they work to create an inclusive culture where everyone feels valued and heard.

Servant leadership: Purpose driven leaders often embody a servant leadership approach, where they prioritize the needs of their team members and stakeholders and work to serve them. They see themselves as facilitators rather than dictators and work to empower others to achieve their goals.

Courage: Purpose driven leaders possess courage and are willing to take bold action in pursuit of their purpose. They are willing to challenge the status quo and take risks in order to achieve their vision.

Transparency: Purpose driven leaders are transparent in their communication and decision-making. They are open and honest with their team members and stakeholders, even when it means delivering difficult news or admitting their own mistakes.

In summary, purpose driven leadership is a highly effective leadership style that is focused on creating a positive impact on society, building strong relationships with stakeholders, and inspiring and motivating others to work towards a shared purpose or vision. Purpose driven leaders possess a range of key characteristics, including decisiveness, emotional intelligence, inclusivity, servant leadership, courage, transparency, and more. By embodying these traits, purpose driven leaders can create a culture of purpose and drive meaningful change in their organizations and communities.

Purpose is a fundamental aspect of human existence, providing direction and meaning to our lives. Purpose can be defined as a sense of direction and motivation that is derived from a deep understanding of what one wants to achieve in life. It is a powerful force that drives individuals and organizations to achieve their goals and create positive change.

For individuals, having a clear sense of purpose can provide a sense of direction and meaning in life. It helps individuals set goals, make decisions, and prioritize their actions based on what is truly important to them. Purpose also provides a sense of fulfillment and satisfaction, as individuals are able to see the impact of their actions on the world around them.

Similarly, purpose is also important for organizations. A clear and compelling purpose can provide a sense of direction and motivation for employees, helping to align their efforts towards a common goal. Purpose also provides a framework for decision-making, helping organizations to prioritize their actions and allocate resources in a way that is consistent with their values and goals.

Leaders play a critical role in shaping and communicating purpose within organizations. They can use purpose to inspire and motivate their employees, creating a shared sense of meaning and direction that drives success and positive change. Leaders can also use purpose to guide strategic decision-making, ensuring that the actions of the organization are aligned with its values and goals.

The importance of purpose can be seen in many different contexts, from individual lives to entire industries. For example, purpose-driven companies are often more successful than those that focus solely on profit. By prioritizing the needs of stakeholders and the wider community, purpose-driven companies are able to build stronger relationships with customers and employees, as well as create a positive impact on society. In turn, this can lead to increased loyalty, brand recognition, and financial success.

Furthermore, purpose can also play a key role in driving innovation and growth. By defining a clear purpose, organizations are able to focus their efforts on solving important problems and creating new opportunities. Purpose can inspire creativity and collaboration, as individuals come together to achieve a shared goal and make a positive impact on the world.

Leaders can use purpose to create a culture of purpose within their organizations. By communicating the organization's purpose in a clear and compelling way, leaders can inspire their employees to work towards a common goal and create a shared sense of meaning and direction. This can lead to increased engagement and motivation, as well as improved performance and job satisfaction.

When individuals have a clear sense of purpose, they are better able to navigate challenges and setbacks, and to persevere in the face of adversity. Purpose provides a sense of meaning and direction that can help individuals stay focused and motivated, even in difficult times. This is particularly important in today's rapidly changing and uncertain world, where individuals may face many challenges and obstacles in their personal and professional lives.

Moreover, purpose can also help individuals find greater meaning and fulfillment in their work. When individuals feel that their work is aligned with their values and goals, they are more likely to be engaged and satisfied with their jobs. Purpose can also help individuals identify their strengths and passions, and to find work that is meaningful and fulfilling.

For organizations, purpose can help attract and retain top talent, as employees are increasingly looking for organizations that align with their values and provide opportunities for meaningful work. Purpose can also help organizations build stronger relationships with customers and stakeholders, as they are able to demonstrate a commitment to making a positive impact on society.

Finally, purpose can be a powerful force for positive change in the world. By aligning their efforts towards a common purpose, individuals and organizations can make a meaningful difference in the lives of others, as well as in the broader society. Purpose can inspire individuals and organizations to take action on important issues, such as social justice, environmental sustainability, and community development.

In summary, purpose is a fundamental aspect of human existence that can drive success, fulfillment, and positive change. By prioritizing purpose in our personal and professional lives, we can find greater meaning and direction, as well as make a meaningful impact on the world around us.

Developing a **personal purpose statement** can be a powerful exercise in clarifying your values, goals, and aspirations. It can serve as a guiding force for your leadership journey by helping you to stay focused on what truly matters to you and by providing a framework for making decisions and taking action.

Here are some steps you can follow to develop your personal purpose statement:

Reflect on your values and beliefs: Start by thinking about the values and beliefs that are most important to you. What motivates you? What do you care deeply about? What principles do you live by?

Identify your strengths and passions: Consider your strengths and passions. What are you good at? What do you enjoy doing? What comes naturally to you?

Think about your vision for the future: Imagine the impact you want to make in the world. What kind of legacy do you want to leave? What do you want to be known for?

Write your purpose statement: Based on your reflections, write a purpose statement that captures your values, strengths, passions, and vision. Your purpose statement should be concise, clear, and actionable. It should inspire you and reflect the best version of yourself.

Review and refine: Review your purpose statement regularly and refine it as needed. As you gain new experiences and insights, your purpose statement may evolve.

Make it specific and actionable: Your purpose statement should be specific and actionable, so that it can guide you in making decisions and taking action. Avoid vague or abstract language that doesn't provide clear direction.

Make it personal: Your purpose statement should reflect your unique values, strengths, passions, and vision. Don't try to copy someone else's purpose statement - it won't feel authentic to you.

Make it aspirational: Your purpose statement should be aspirational, meaning it should reflect the best version of yourself and the impact you want to make. Don't limit yourself by thinking small - aim high!

Share it with others: Sharing your purpose statement with others can help you to build alignment and accountability. Consider sharing it with your team, mentor, or trusted friends and family members.

Use it as a compass, not a destination: Remember that your purpose statement is a guiding force, not a destination. It can help you to stay focused on what matters most to you, but it won't solve all your problems or answer all your questions. Be open to new experiences and insights that may challenge or refine your purpose statement over time.

Make it adaptable: Your purpose statement should be adaptable, meaning it can evolve over time as you gain new experiences and insights. Don't be afraid to revise your purpose statement if it no longer resonates with you or if you have a new vision for your future.

Use it to set goals: Your purpose statement can be a powerful tool for setting goals that align with your values and vision. Use it to guide your goal-setting process and ensure that your goals are meaningful and impactful.

Use it to prioritize: Your purpose statement can also help you to prioritize your time and energy. When faced with competing demands, ask yourself which option aligns best with your purpose statement and will have the greatest impact.

Use it to inspire others: Your purpose statement can also inspire others to join you on your journey. Share your purpose statement with your team, colleagues, or followers to inspire them and build alignment around a shared vision.

Review it regularly: Finally, make sure to review your purpose statement regularly to ensure that it continues to reflect your values and aspirations. Set aside time to reflect on your progress, refine your goals, and make any necessary updates to your purpose statement.

Align it with your organization's mission: If you are a leader within an organization, it can be helpful to align your personal purpose statement with the organization's mission and values. This can help to build alignment and create a shared sense of purpose among team members.

Use it to make tough decisions: Your purpose statement can be a powerful tool for making tough decisions. When faced with a difficult choice, ask yourself which option aligns best with your purpose statement and will help you to make the greatest impact.

Keep it visible: Keep your purpose statement visible to remind yourself of your values and vision. Write it down and post it in a prominent location, or create a visual representation that you can refer to regularly.

Use it to stay motivated: Your purpose statement can also help you to stay motivated during challenging times. When faced with setbacks or obstacles, remind yourself of your purpose and the impact you want to make.

Embrace the journey: Finally, remember that developing a personal purpose statement is a journey, not a destination. Embrace the process of self-discovery and be open to new experiences and insights that may shape your purpose statement over time.

Aligning personal and organizational purpose is important for several reasons. First, when individuals feel that their personal values and goals align with those of the organization, they are more likely to be motivated and engaged in their work. This can lead to increased productivity, job satisfaction, and retention.

Second, when an organization's purpose is clearly defined and communicated, it can attract individuals who share that purpose and are more likely to be committed to the organization's success. This can lead to a more cohesive and high-performing team.

To achieve alignment between personal and organizational purpose, there are a few key steps that can be taken:

Clearly define the organization's purpose: This involves identifying the mission, vision, and values of the organization, and communicating them clearly to all stakeholders.

Encourage employees to identify their personal purpose: This involves helping individuals to reflect on their own values, interests, and goals, and how they align with those of the organization.

Connect the dots: This involves identifying the ways in which an individual's personal purpose can be fulfilled through their work within the organization. This can involve creating opportunities for employees to work on projects that align with their personal interests, or providing training and development opportunities that support their career goals.

Foster a culture of purpose: This involves creating an environment where purpose is valued and celebrated. This can involve recognizing and rewarding individuals who demonstrate a strong commitment to the organization's purpose, and providing opportunities for employees to contribute to the development and implementation of the organization's purpose.

Provide opportunities for feedback: Employees should be given the opportunity to provide feedback on the organization's purpose and how it aligns with their personal goals. This can help to identify areas where alignment may be lacking and provide opportunities for improvement.

Encourage collaboration and teamwork: By fostering a culture of collaboration and teamwork, individuals can work together to achieve a common purpose and contribute to the success of the organization. This can also provide opportunities for individuals to learn from one another and develop new skills.

Support work-life balance: Individuals who feel that their personal life and values are respected and supported by the organization are more likely to feel engaged and committed to their work. Providing flexible work arrangements and support for work-life balance can help to achieve this alignment.

Communicate consistently and transparently: It is important to communicate the organization's purpose consistently and transparently to all stakeholders, including employees, customers, and partners. This can help to build trust and credibility, and ensure that everyone is working towards a common goal.

Lead by example: Leaders should model the organization's purpose and values in their own behavior and decision- making. This can help to build trust and credibility, and inspire others to do the same.

Provide opportunities for personal growth: Individuals who feel that they are growing and developing within their roles are more likely to feel engaged and committed to their work. Providing opportunities for training, mentoring, and career development can help to achieve this alignment.

Foster a sense of community: By creating a sense of community within the organization, individuals can feel that they are part of something larger than themselves and that their contributions are valued. This can be achieved through team-building activities, social events, and other initiatives that bring employees together.

Celebrate successes: Recognizing and celebrating successes can help to reinforce the organization's purpose and values, and create a sense of pride and accomplishment among employees.

Use technology to support alignment: Technology can be used to support alignment between personal and organizational purpose by providing tools and resources that facilitate communication, collaboration, and development. For example, a learning management system can be used to provide training and development opportunities, while a social intranet can be used to facilitate communication and collaboration.

Be flexible and adaptable: Finally, it is important to be flexible and adaptable in the pursuit of alignment between personal and organizational purpose. As the organization's purpose evolves and individuals' personal goals and interests change, it may be necessary to adjust strategies and initiatives to ensure that alignment is maintained.

Encourage innovation and creativity: Providing opportunities for individuals to be creative and innovative in their work can help to foster a sense of purpose and meaning. This can involve encouraging individuals to propose new ideas and solutions, or providing resources and support for innovation initiatives.

Build trust and psychological safety: Individuals are more likely to feel aligned with the organization's purpose when they feel that they are part of a trusting and supportive environment. Building trust and psychological safety can involve creating an environment where individuals feel comfortable speaking up, taking risks, and making mistakes.

Provide opportunities for social impact: Individuals who feel that their work is making a positive impact on society are more likely to feel aligned with the organization's purpose. Providing opportunities for social impact can involve initiatives such as corporate social responsibility programs, volunteer opportunities, or partnerships with community organizations.

Measure and track alignment: Finally, it is important to measure and track alignment between personal and organizational purpose to ensure that progress is being made. This can involve tracking employee engagement and satisfaction, as well as measuring the impact of initiatives designed to foster alignment.

By adopting these additional strategies, organizations can create a culture that is aligned with its purpose, fostering a sense of meaning and purpose among employees, and achieving greater success over the long term.

Effective communication is indeed crucial for purpose-driven leadership, as it allows leaders to articulate their vision and inspire others to work towards a common goal. Communicating a purpose in a way that inspires and motivates others requires a clear understanding of the purpose, the audience, and the most effective communication channels.

To communicate a purpose effectively, leaders should start by clearly defining the purpose and its relevance to the organization and its stakeholders. This involves identifying the key values and principles that underpin the purpose, as well as the specific goals and objectives that it aims to achieve.

Once the purpose has been defined, leaders should tailor their communication to the audience they are addressing. This means considering factors such as their level of knowledge and expertise, their interests and concerns, and their communication preferences. For example, if the audience is composed of technical experts, the leader may need to provide more detailed information about the purpose and its implementation, whereas if the audience is composed of stakeholders with diverse backgrounds, the leader may need to use more accessible language and provide more context and examples.

Finally, leaders should choose the most effective communication channels to reach their audience. This may include face-to-face meetings, presentations, emails, social media, and other forms of communication. The choice of channel will depend on factors such as the size and location of the audience, the level of interactivity required, and the urgency of the message.

Use storytelling: People are more likely to remember and be inspired by stories than by facts and figures. Leaders can use storytelling to illustrate the impact of their purpose on real people and situations, and to create an emotional connection with their audience.

Be authentic: Authenticity is key to building trust and credibility with your audience. Leaders should communicate their purpose in a way that reflects their own values and beliefs, and avoid using jargon or language that feels insincere or inauthentic.

Provide context: To help their audience understand the purpose and its importance, leaders should provide context and background information. This could include explaining the history of the organization, the current challenges it faces, and the opportunities that the purpose presents.

Repeat the message: People need to hear a message multiple times in order to remember it and take action on it. Leaders should repeat their purpose message regularly, using different channels and formats, to ensure that it stays top of mind for their audience.

Encourage feedback: Communication is a two-way process, and leaders should encourage feedback and questions from their audience to ensure that the purpose is understood and embraced. This can help to identify any misunderstandings or concerns, and provide an opportunity to address them and build buy-in for the purpose.

Be concise: People have a limited attention span and are more likely to remember short, simple messages. Leaders should aim to communicate their purpose in a concise and straightforward way, focusing on the key points and avoiding unnecessary details.

Use visual aids: Visual aids such as diagrams, charts, and infographics can help to convey complex information in a clear and engaging way. Leaders should use visual aids to support their message, and ensure that they are easy to understand and visually appealing.

Use examples: Examples can help to bring the purpose to life and show how it can be applied in practice. Leaders should use real-world examples, case studies, and success stories to illustrate the impact of the purpose and inspire their audience.

Be inclusive: To ensure that the purpose is embraced by everyone in the organization, leaders should communicate it in an inclusive way that reflects the diversity of their audience. This could involve using language that is gender- neutral, avoiding cultural stereotypes, and being sensitive to the needs and perspectives of different groups.

Lead by example: Leaders should lead by example and embody the purpose in their own behavior and actions. This can help to build trust and credibility with their audience, and demonstrate the importance of the purpose in practice.

Be passionate: Passion is contagious and can help to inspire and motivate others. Leaders should communicate their purpose with enthusiasm and conviction, and show that they truly believe in its importance and potential impact.

Involve others: To build buy-in and commitment for the purpose, leaders should involve others in the process of defining and communicating it. This could involve soliciting feedback from stakeholders, creating opportunities for dialogue and discussion, and co-creating the purpose with others.

Address objections: Not everyone will immediately embrace the purpose, and leaders should be prepared to address objections and concerns. This could involve anticipating potential objections and providing responses in advance, or creating opportunities for open discussion and debate.

Create a sense of urgency: To motivate action and create momentum for the purpose, leaders should create a sense of urgency around it. This could involve highlighting the risks and opportunities associated with the purpose, or setting ambitious goals and timelines for its implementation.

Measure progress: To ensure that the purpose is making a real impact, leaders should measure progress and communicate it regularly. This could involve tracking key performance indicators, sharing success stories, and celebrating milestones and achievements along the way.

Be transparent: Transparency is essential for building trust and credibility with your audience. Leaders should be transparent about the purpose, including its goals, objectives, and implementation plan, as well as any challenges or risks associated with it.

Be consistent: Consistency is key to ensuring that the purpose is understood and embraced by everyone in the organization. Leaders should communicate the purpose consistently across all channels and platforms, and ensure that everyone is using the same language and messaging.

Engage with stakeholders: To ensure that the purpose is relevant and meaningful to stakeholders, leaders should engage with them throughout the process. This could involve soliciting feedback, hosting stakeholder meetings, and creating opportunities for collaboration and co-creation.

Use humor: Humor can be a powerful tool for engaging and inspiring others. Leaders should use humor in a way that is appropriate and relevant to their audience, and that helps to create a positive and upbeat atmosphere.

Be adaptable: Communication needs and preferences may vary depending on the situation and the audience. Leaders should be adaptable and willing to adjust their communication style and approach as needed to ensure that the purpose is effectively communicated and understood.

Creating a **purpose-driven culture** is essential for organizations that want to thrive in today's business landscape. A purpose-driven culture is one where employees are engaged and motivated because they feel connected to the organization's mission and values. Leaders play a critical role in creating and nurturing such a culture.

To create a purpose-driven culture, leaders need to start by defining the organization's purpose. This purpose should be clear, concise, and inspiring. It should provide a sense of direction and meaning for employees, and it should be aligned with the organization's values and goals.

Once the purpose is defined, leaders need to communicate it effectively to their employees. This means not just telling employees what the purpose is but also demonstrating how it is being lived out in the organization's day-to- day operations. Leaders should also encourage employees to share their own ideas and perspectives on how the purpose can be better integrated into the organization's culture.

Another critical aspect of creating a purpose-driven culture is to align the organization's goals and objectives with its purpose. This means that everything the organization does, from strategic planning to day-to-day decision-making, should be guided by its purpose. Leaders should ensure that all employees understand how their work contributes to the organization's purpose and that they have the resources and support they need to fulfill their roles.

Finally, leaders should recognize and reward employees who demonstrate behaviors that support the organization's purpose. This can be done through formal recognition programs, such as employee of the month awards, or through informal recognition, such as public praise or a simple thank you.

In summary, creating a purpose-driven culture requires leaders to define the organization's purpose, communicate it effectively, align goals and objectives with purpose, and recognize and reward behaviors that support purpose. By doing so, leaders can create a culture that supports purpose and meaningful work, which can lead to increased employee engagement, productivity, and organizational success.

Lead by example: Leaders need to embody the organization's purpose and values. They should be role models for their employees and demonstrate how the purpose is being lived out in their own actions and behaviors.

Foster collaboration and teamwork: A purpose-driven culture requires collaboration and teamwork across all levels of the organization. Leaders should encourage employees to work together and break down silos to achieve common goals.

Provide opportunities for growth and development: Employees who feel supported and invested in are more likely to be engaged and motivated. Leaders should provide opportunities for growth and development, such as training and mentoring programs, to help employees develop their skills and advance their careers.

Create a positive work environment: A positive work environment is essential for creating a purpose-driven culture. Leaders should foster a workplace culture that promotes positivity, respect, and inclusivity.

Measure progress: To ensure that the organization is staying true to its purpose, leaders should regularly measure progress and evaluate how well the organization is fulfilling its purpose. This can be done through surveys, feedback sessions, and other forms of data collection.

Encourage innovation and risk-taking: Purpose-driven cultures are often characterized by a willingness to take risks and try new things. Leaders should encourage employees to innovate and experiment, and provide them with the resources and support they need to do so.

Foster open communication: Open communication is essential for creating a purpose-driven culture. Leaders should encourage employees to share their ideas and perspectives, and be transparent about the organization's goals and objectives.

Recognize the importance of work-life balance: A purpose-driven culture should support employees' overall well- being, both inside and outside of work. Leaders should recognize the importance of work-life balance and provide employees with the flexibility they need to manage their personal and professional responsibilities.

Embrace diversity and inclusion: A purpose-driven culture should be inclusive of all employees, regardless of their background, identity, or beliefs. Leaders should embrace diversity and foster a culture of inclusion, where all employees feel valued and respected.

Celebrate successes: Celebrating successes is a crucial component of creating a purpose-driven culture. Leaders should acknowledge and celebrate the achievements of individuals and teams, and recognize the impact of their work on the organization's purpose.

Ultimately, creating a purpose-driven culture requires a long-term commitment from leaders and all employees. By cultivating a culture that supports purpose and meaningful work, organizations can create a competitive advantage, attract top talent, and achieve long-term success.

Involve employees in the process: To create a purpose-driven culture, it's important to involve employees in the process. Leaders should gather input from employees and encourage them to share their thoughts and ideas about the organization's purpose and values. This can help ensure that the purpose is meaningful and relevant to everyone in the organization.

Provide ongoing training and development: Creating a purpose-driven culture requires ongoing training and development to reinforce the organization's purpose and values. Leaders should provide regular training and development opportunities to help employees understand and embody the purpose and values of the organization.

Set clear expectations: Leaders should set clear expectations for employees and hold them accountable for living out the organization's purpose and values. This can be achieved through performance evaluations, feedback, and recognition programs.

Encourage autonomy: Employees who feel empowered and trusted are more likely to be engaged and committed to the organization's purpose. Leaders should encourage autonomy and give employees the freedom to make decisions and take ownership of their work.

Lead with empathy: Creating a purpose-driven culture requires leaders who are empathetic and understanding. Leaders should take the time to listen to their employees and understand their perspectives, needs, and concerns. This can help build trust and create a more supportive and collaborative work environment.

In summary, creating a purpose-driven culture requires a collective effort from leaders and employees. By involving employees in the process, providing ongoing training and development, setting clear expectations, encouraging autonomy, and leading with empathy, leaders can create a culture that supports purpose and meaningful work, and ultimately drive success for their organization.

Leading with values is a critical aspect of purpose-driven leadership. Values serve as the foundation for your leadership style, and they guide your decision-making process, helping you to stay focused on what is important to you and your organization.

To identify your values as a leader, you may want to start by reflecting on your personal and professional experiences. Think about the times when you felt most fulfilled and engaged in your work, and consider what values were present in those situations. Additionally, you may want to consider the values of your organization and how they align with your personal values.

Once you have identified your values, it is important to prioritize them. You may find that some values are more important to you than others, and it is important to be clear about which values take precedence in your decision- making process.

Using your values to guide your decision-making process can help you to stay true to your core beliefs and principles, even in challenging situations. When faced with difficult decisions, you can refer back to your values to help you determine the best course of action.

It is also important to communicate your values to your team and stakeholders. By being transparent about your values and how they guide your decision-making process, you can build trust and inspire others to align with your vision and mission.

Continuously reassess your values: Your values may evolve over time, so it is important to regularly reassess them and ensure they still align with your personal and professional goals and the goals of your organization.

Lead by example: As a leader, you set the tone for your team. By consistently demonstrating your values in your actions and decisions, you can inspire your team to adopt those same values and behaviors.

Use your values to build a strong company culture: Your values can help shape the culture of your organization. By articulating and promoting your values, you can create a shared sense of purpose and direction that can help align your team and drive success.

Be open to feedback: Solicit feedback from your team and stakeholders on how you are embodying your values and whether there are areas where you could improve. This can help you stay accountable and continue to grow as a leader.

Embrace diversity and inclusion: Your values should be inclusive and reflect a commitment to diversity, equity, inclusion, and belonging. By embracing and valuing diversity, you can build a more resilient and innovative organization that draws on a wider range of perspectives and experiences.

Stay true to your values in challenging situations: When faced with difficult decisions, it can be tempting to compromise your values to achieve a desired outcome. However, staying true to your values, even when it's hard, is essential for building trust and credibility with your team and stakeholders.

Clearly communicate your values: Make sure your team and stakeholders understand your values and how they inform your decision-making process. This can help build trust and ensure everyone is aligned on the organization's direction.

Align your actions with your values: Your actions should reflect your values. Make sure your decisions and behaviors are consistent with the values you have identified.

Encourage feedback from your team: Encourage your team to provide feedback on how you are embodying your values, and listen to their perspectives. This can help you identify blind spots and areas where you can improve.

Recognize and celebrate values-based behavior: When you see your team members demonstrating values-based behavior, recognize and celebrate it. This can help reinforce the importance of your values and inspire others to embody them as well.

Continuously learn and grow: Leading with values is an ongoing process of growth and learning. Stay open to feedback and be willing to make adjustments as needed to ensure your values remain aligned with your personal and organizational goals.

Make values-based decisions: Use your values to guide your decision-making process. When faced with a difficult decision, consider how each option aligns with your values, and choose the option that best supports them.

Incorporate values into your goals: Incorporate your values into your personal and organizational goals. This can help ensure that you are working towards outcomes that are aligned with your values.

Hire and promote based on values: When hiring and promoting team members, consider their alignment with your values. Look for candidates who embody your values and are likely to contribute to a positive and values-driven culture.

Be consistent: Consistency is key in leading with values. Make sure your actions and decisions are consistent with your values, even in situations where it may be tempting to compromise.

Continuously communicate your values: Regularly communicate your values to your team and stakeholders, and demonstrate how they inform your actions and decisions. This can help keep everyone aligned on the organization's direction and build a culture of trust and purpose.

Be accountable: Hold yourself accountable to your values, and hold your team accountable as well. This can help ensure that everyone is working towards a shared vision and aligned with the organization's values.

In summary, leading with values requires a commitment to incorporating your values into all aspects of your leadership, from decision-making to goal-setting to hiring and promoting. By embodying your values and consistently communicating them to your team, you can build a strong and values-driven organization.

A clear and compelling vision is the foundation of purpose-driven leadership. It helps to define the purpose and direction of the organization or team, and serves as a guide for decision-making and goal setting. A strong vision inspires and motivates others to join you on your journey, and helps to create a sense of shared purpose and commitment.

Here are a few steps to creating a vision:

Start with your purpose: A vision should be aligned with your organization's purpose. Ask yourself, what is the ultimate goal of your organization? What is the impact you want to make in the world? Use this purpose as the foundation for your vision.

Envision the future: Think about what you want your organization to look like in the future. What will be different? What will be better? What will you have accomplished? Imagine the ideal state of your organization and use this as inspiration for your vision.

Make it clear and concise: Your vision should be easy to understand and communicate. Use clear language and keep it concise. Your vision should be something that can be easily remembered and repeated.

Make it aspirational: Your vision should be ambitious and aspirational. It should inspire people to strive for greatness and be motivated to achieve something bigger than themselves.

Be inclusive: Involve your team in the process of creating the vision. Ask for their input and ideas. This will help to create a shared sense of ownership and commitment to the vision.

Make it actionable: Your vision should be something that can be turned into actionable goals and plans. It should guide decision-making and help to prioritize initiatives.

Be authentic: Your vision should be authentic and reflective of your organization's values, culture, and personality. It should be something that your team and stakeholders can relate to and feel passionate about.

Use storytelling: Use storytelling to bring your vision to life. Share stories of how your organization has made a difference in people's lives or how you plan to make a difference in the future. This will help to create an emotional connection to your vision.

Focus on the benefits: Your vision should focus on the benefits that your organization will bring to others. Think about how your organization will make the world a better place and communicate this in your vision.

Test your vision: Test your vision with your team and stakeholders to make sure it resonates with them. Ask for feedback and make adjustments as necessary.

Be flexible: Be open to adjusting your vision if necessary. As your organization evolves and changes, your vision may need to be revised to reflect new priorities or goals.

Lead by example: As a purpose-driven leader, you should embody your vision and lead by example. Your actions and decisions should be guided by your vision and demonstrate your commitment to it.

Be bold: Don't be afraid to think big and be bold with your vision. A bold vision can inspire people to take action and achieve great things.

Keep it simple: While your vision should be bold, it should also be simple and easy to understand. Avoid using jargon or complex language that can confuse or alienate people.

Use visuals: Visuals can be a powerful tool for communicating your vision. Use images, videos, or infographics to help bring your vision to life and make it more memorable.

Align your actions: Your vision should guide your actions and decisions. Make sure that everything you do, from hiring to strategic planning, is aligned with your vision.

Celebrate progress: Celebrate progress towards your vision to keep your team motivated and engaged. Recognize and reward individuals and teams that are making a meaningful contribution towards achieving your vision.

Communicate frequently: Communicate your vision frequently and consistently. Use all available channels, from company meetings to social media, to keep your team and stakeholders informed and engaged.

Be optimistic: Your vision should be optimistic and focus on the positive change your organization can bring to the world. Avoid negative or fear-based messaging, which can create a sense of hopelessness and discourage action.

Be inclusive: Ensure that your vision is inclusive and reflects the diversity of your team and stakeholders. Consider how your vision can benefit all members of your organization and society as a whole.

Be persistent: Creating a compelling vision takes time and effort, and it may take some time for your team and stakeholders to fully embrace it. Be persistent and continue to communicate and reinforce your vision over time.

Measure progress: Set key performance indicators (KPIs) to measure progress towards your vision. This will help you track your progress and identify areas for improvement.

Stay true to your values: Your vision should be aligned with your organization's values and culture. Ensure that your vision reflects your core values and that you stay true to them as you work towards achieving your goals.

Be open to feedback: Be open to feedback from your team and stakeholders on your vision. This can help you identify areas for improvement and refine your vision over time.

Stay focused: Your vision should be the guiding force behind all of your organization's activities. Stay focused on your vision and avoid getting sidetracked by distractions or short-term goals that don't align with your long-term vision.

Creating a compelling vision is a critical component of purpose-driven leadership. By following these tips, you can create a vision that inspires and motivates your team to achieve great things and make a meaningful impact in the world.

Taking purposeful action is essential to achieving one's goals and bringing their vision to life. Here are some tips that can help you take purposeful action and overcome obstacles:

Define your goals and vision: Before taking action, it's important to have a clear understanding of what you want to achieve and why it matters to you. Take some time to reflect on your goals and vision, and write them down. This will help you stay focused and motivated as you take action.

Break it down: Once you have defined your goals and vision, break them down into smaller, actionable steps. This will make the process less overwhelming and help you make progress towards your goals.

Create a plan: Once you have a list of actionable steps, create a plan to move forward. Set deadlines for each step and prioritize them based on their importance and urgency.

Take action: Now it's time to take action! Start with the first step on your list and work your way through it. Don't get bogged down by perfectionism or fear of failure. Remember that taking imperfect action is better than taking no action at all.

Stay motivated: As you take action, it's important to stay motivated and focused on your goals. Celebrate your successes along the way, and don't be too hard on yourself if things don't go according to plan. Use setbacks as an opportunity to learn and grow.

Overcome obstacles: Along the way, you may face obstacles that threaten to derail your progress. Don't give up! Instead, use these obstacles as an opportunity to problem-solve and find new ways forward. Remember that obstacles are a natural part of the process, and they can often lead to unexpected breakthroughs.

Stay accountable: One of the best ways to stay on track and take purposeful action is to stay accountable. Share your goals and plans with someone you trust, such as a friend, family member, or mentor.

This person can provide support and encouragement, and hold you accountable when you need it.

Stay flexible: While it's important to have a plan and take action, it's also important to stay flexible. Be open to new ideas and opportunities that may arise along the way, and be willing to adjust your plan as needed.

Practice self-care: Taking purposeful action towards your goals can be a challenging and sometimes stressful process. That's why it's important to practice self-care and prioritize your well-being. Make time for rest, relaxation, and activities that bring you joy and fulfillment.

Learn from others: Finally, don't be afraid to learn from others who have achieved similar goals or overcome similar obstacles. Seek out mentors or role models who can offer guidance and support, and learn from their experiences.

Visualize success: Visualization is a powerful tool that can help you stay motivated and focused on your goals. Take some time each day to visualize yourself achieving your goals and experiencing the success you desire. This can help you stay motivated and focused on taking purposeful action towards your goals.

Embrace failure: Failure is a natural part of the process of taking purposeful action towards your goals. Don't be afraid of it! Instead, embrace failure as an opportunity to learn and grow. Analyze what went wrong, and use that information to adjust your approach and take more purposeful action moving forward.

Stay positive: Maintaining a positive attitude can make a big difference when it comes to taking purposeful action and overcoming obstacles. Focus on the progress you've made, celebrate your successes, and stay optimistic about the future.

Stay organized: Finally, staying organized can help you stay on track and take purposeful action towards your goals. Use tools like calendars, to-do lists, and project management software to keep track of your progress and stay organized.

Stay committed: Taking purposeful action towards your goals requires commitment. Stay committed to your goals and vision, even when the going gets tough. Remind yourself of why your goals are important to you, and stay focused on the bigger picture.

Get feedback: Getting feedback from others can help you improve and make progress towards your goals. Seek out feedback from trusted friends, family members, or mentors, and use that feedback to adjust your approach and take more purposeful action.

Take breaks: Taking purposeful action requires energy and focus. Make sure to take breaks and recharge your batteries as needed. This can help you stay motivated and avoid burnout.

Celebrate progress: Celebrating progress along the way can help you stay motivated and focused on your goals. Take time to celebrate your successes and acknowledge the progress you've made, no matter how small.

Learn from mistakes: Mistakes are a natural part of the process of taking purposeful action. Instead of dwelling on your mistakes, use them as an opportunity to learn and grow. Analyze what went wrong, and use that information to adjust your approach and take more purposeful action moving forward.

Take responsibility: Finally, taking purposeful action requires taking responsibility for your actions and outcomes. Don't blame others or external factors for your lack of progress. Instead, take responsibility for your actions and outcomes, and focus on what you can control.

Remember, taking purposeful action towards your goals is a journey that requires patience, persistence, and determination. Keep these tips in mind, stay focused on your goals, and keep moving forward, even when the going gets tough.

Failure is an integral part of any leadership journey. It is through failure that we learn, grow, and improve. As a purpose-driven leader, it is important to embrace failure as a learning opportunity and use it to propel you and your team forward. In this chapter, we will explore how to embrace failure, learn from it, and ultimately turn it into a success.

Redefining Failure

The first step in embracing failure is to redefine it. Instead of seeing failure as something negative, view it as an opportunity to learn and grow. By changing your mindset around failure, you will be better equipped to handle setbacks and use them to your advantage.

Encouraging a Culture of Learning

As a leader, it is crucial to create an environment where failure is seen as a valuable learning experience. Encourage your team to take risks, try new things, and learn from their mistakes. By fostering a culture of learning, you will promote innovation and creativity within your organization.

The Power of Reflection

Reflection is an essential part of learning from failure. Take the time to analyze the situation, identify the root cause of the failure, and determine what can be done differently in the future. By reflecting on your experiences, you can gain valuable insights and develop strategies for improvement.

Embracing Vulnerability

Being open and honest about your failures can be a powerful way to connect with your team and build trust. Share your own experiences with failure and demonstrate that it is a normal part of the leadership journey. By embracing vulnerability, you will encourage your team to do the same, fostering a culture of openness and collaboration.

Learning from Others

There is much to be learned from the experiences of others. Seek out opportunities to learn from other leaders who have faced failure and grown from it. Attend workshops, read books, and listen to podcasts to gain insights and perspectives on how to embrace failure and turn it into success.

Adapting and Growing

Failure provides an opportunity to adapt and grow. Use the lessons learned from your failures to make improvements to your processes, strategies, and leadership style. By continuously adapting and growing, you will become a more resilient and effective leader.

Building Resilience

Resilience is the ability to bounce back from failure and continue moving forward. As you embrace failure and learn from it, you will naturally develop greater resilience. Encourage your team to develop this skill as well, by providing support and guidance during challenging times. The more resilient your team is, the better equipped you will be to face future challenges and setbacks.

Celebrating Successes and Learning from Failure

One way to create a balanced perspective on failure is to celebrate successes while also acknowledging and learning from failures. When your team achieves a goal or milestone, take the time to recognize their hard work and dedication. At the same time, encourage open communication about any setbacks or challenges experienced along the way. This approach will reinforce the importance of learning from failure and create a more positive, supportive work environment.

Developing a Growth Mindset

A growth mindset is the belief that abilities and intelligence can be developed through hard work, dedication, and learning from failures. Cultivate a growth mindset in yourself and your team by encouraging continuous learning, embracing challenges, and praising effort rather than just outcomes. By fostering a growth mindset, you will empower your team to overcome setbacks and achieve their full potential.

Implementing a System for Continuous Improvement

Establish a system for continuous improvement within your organization to ensure that lessons learned from failure are put into practice. This can include regular check-ins with your team, setting benchmarks for progress, and creating a feedback loop to help identify areas for improvement. By implementing a structured approach to continuous improvement, you can transform failure into an opportunity for growth and development.

Encouraging Creativity and Innovation

Fostering a work environment that encourages creativity and innovation can help you and your team find new solutions to problems and prevent repeating the same mistakes. Provide the necessary resources, tools, and encouragement for your team to think outside the box and explore new ideas. By promoting a culture of innovation, you can turn failure into a catalyst for positive change and growth.

Seeking Feedback and Constructive Criticism

Actively seeking feedback and constructive criticism from your team, peers, and mentors can provide valuable insights into areas where you may need to improve. By being open to feedback and willing to make adjustments, you demonstrate your commitment to learning from your failures and becoming a better leader.

Understanding the Importance of Emotional Intelligence

Emotional intelligence plays a crucial role in embracing failure and learning from it. Developing your emotional intelligence can help you better manage your emotions in times of setbacks and provide support and empathy to your team members when they experience failure. By cultivating emotional intelligence, you can create stronger connections within your team and foster a more supportive work environment.

Setting Realistic Expectations

While it's essential to set ambitious goals, it's also important to recognize that failure is a natural part of the process. By setting realistic expectations for yourself and your team, you create an environment where failure is viewed as a learning opportunity rather than a cause for disappointment or blame. This approach can help boost morale and encourage your team to take risks and learn from their experiences.

Analyzing Failure Patterns

Over time, you may notice patterns in the types of failures that occur within your team or organization. By analyzing these patterns, you can identify potential systemic issues or areas for improvement. Addressing these underlying causes of failure can help prevent future setbacks and improve overall performance.

Conclusion

Embracing failure is a crucial component of effective leadership and long-term success. By fostering an environment that encourages creativity, innovation, and emotional intelligence, you can turn failure into an opportunity for growth and development. By actively seeking feedback, setting realistic expectations, and analyzing failure patterns, you can make continuous improvements and become a more effective and resilient leader. By embracing and learning from failure, you will be better equipped to lead your team to success and drive meaningful progress.

Empathy is the ability to understand and share the feelings of others. It is a key skill for purpose-driven leaders who aim to connect with their team members and create a supportive work environment. Leading with empathy means not only understanding the emotions and experiences of others, but also responding with compassion and support. This chapter will explore the importance of empathy in leadership, how to cultivate empathy, and how to apply it to build strong relationships with your team.

The Importance of Empathy in Leadership

Empathy is essential for effective leadership because it enables leaders to:

- Build trust: Empathy helps leaders understand and validate the emotions of their team members, which fosters trust and loyalty.
- Improve communication: Being empathetic allows leaders to communicate more effectively by understanding the perspectives and emotions of others.
- Enhance collaboration: Empathy promotes a collaborative work environment, as team members feel understood and respected.
- Boost team morale: When leaders demonstrate empathy, team members feel supported and valued, which can improve overall morale and job satisfaction.

Cultivating Empathy

Developing empathy requires practice and self-awareness. Here are some steps to cultivate empathy:

- Practice active listening: Pay full attention to what others are saying, without interrupting or formulating a response while they are speaking.

- Observe non-verbal cues: Be aware of body language, facial expressions, and tone of voice, which can provide valuable insights into how others are feeling.
- Develop self-awareness: Reflect on your own emotions and experiences to better understand those of others.
- Ask open-ended questions: Encourage others to share their feelings and thoughts by asking questions that promote discussion.
- Express empathy: Let others know that you understand and acknowledge their emotions.

Applying Empathy to Build Strong Relationships with Your Team

To lead with empathy and build strong relationships with your team, consider the following strategies:

- Create a supportive environment: Encourage open communication and provide a safe space for team members to express their feelings and concerns.
- Be approachable: Make yourself available to your team and be willing to engage in conversations about their experiences and emotions.
- Acknowledge individual needs: Recognize and address the unique needs of each team member, and be flexible in your approach to accommodate them.
- Offer support and encouragement: Provide guidance, resources, and encouragement to help team members overcome challenges and achieve their goals.

Empathy and Emotional Intelligence

Developing empathy is closely related to enhancing emotional intelligence (EI). EI is the ability to recognize, understand, and manage our own emotions and the emotions of others. It consists of four main components:

- Self-awareness: Being aware of your own emotions and understanding how they impact your behavior and decision-making.
- Self-management: The ability to regulate your emotions and respond appropriately in different situations.
- Social awareness: Recognizing and understanding the emotions of others, which includes empathy.
- Relationship management: Using emotional understanding to build and maintain strong relationships with others.

By enhancing your emotional intelligence, you can become a more empathetic leader, improving your ability to connect with and support your team.

Empathy in Conflict Resolution

Conflicts are inevitable in any team. Leading with empathy can help resolve conflicts more effectively by:

- Encouraging open communication: Create an environment where team members feel comfortable expressing their concerns and emotions.
- Understanding different perspectives: Use empathy to understand the feelings and viewpoints of each individual involved in the conflict.
- Finding common ground: Identify shared interests and goals to help bridge the gap between conflicting parties.
- Collaboratively problem solving: Work together with the

conflicting parties to develop solutions that address their concerns and foster a positive outcome.

Empathy and Diversity and Inclusion

An empathetic leader is well-positioned to promote diversity and inclusion within their team. To do this:

- Be aware of unconscious biases: Recognize your own biases and work to overcome them to ensure fair treatment of all team members.
- Encourage open dialogue: Foster an environment where team members can share their experiences and perspectives related to diversity and inclusion.
- Value different opinions: Recognize the value of diverse perspectives and encourage team members to contribute their unique ideas and opinions.
- Provide equal opportunities: Ensure that all team members have equal access to resources, support, and opportunities for growth and advancement.

Empathy and Remote Work

With the rise of remote work, empathetic leadership becomes even more crucial. Here are some ways to lead with empathy in a remote setting:

- Regular check-ins: Schedule consistent one-on-one meetings with your team members to discuss their well-being, workload, and any concerns.
- Encourage work-life balance: Be understanding of the challenges remote workers face, and support them in maintaining a healthy work-life balance.
- Foster connection: Create opportunities for team

members to connect and engage with each other, such as virtual team-building activities or casual video conferences.

Empathy and Employee Development

Empathetic leaders play a crucial role in the personal and professional growth of their team members. To support employee development, empathetic leaders should:

- Understand individual goals and aspirations: Engage in conversations to learn about the career ambitions and personal goals of your team members.
- Provide constructive feedback: Offer balanced, specific, and actionable feedback that helps team members grow and improve.
- Empower employees: Encourage team members to take on new challenges and responsibilities that align with their interests and goals.
- Offer mentoring and coaching: Provide guidance, share knowledge, and help team members navigate challenges in their careers.

Empathy and Decision-Making

Empathetic leaders can make more informed and balanced decisions by considering the feelings and perspectives of their team members. When making decisions, empathetic leaders should:

- Consult with the team: Seek input from team members to understand their opinions, concerns, and suggestions.
- Consider the impact on people: Evaluate the potential consequences of a decision on the well-being, workload, and morale of your team.

- Communicate openly: Transparently share the reasons behind a decision and discuss how it aligns with the team's goals and values.
- Be open to feedback: Encourage team members to voice their thoughts about a decision and be willing to adjust your course of action if necessary.

Empathy and Resilience

Leading with empathy can also foster resilience within your team. Resilience is the ability to adapt to challenges and bounce back from setbacks. To promote resilience, empathetic leaders can:

- Model resilient behavior: Demonstrate how to cope with stress and setbacks in a healthy and constructive way.
- Provide support during challenges: Offer guidance, resources, and encouragement to help team members navigate difficult situations.
- Foster a growth mindset: Encourage team members to view challenges as opportunities for growth and learning.
- Celebrate progress and learning: Acknowledge the efforts and progress your team makes, even in the face of setbacks.

In conclusion, by incorporating empathy into various aspects of leadership, such as employee development, decision-making, and promoting resilience, you can create a supportive and collaborative work environment that enables your team to grow, adapt, and achieve its full potential. Empathetic leadership is an indispensable skill for purpose-driven leaders who seek to understand, connect with, and support their team members.

Leadership is an indispensable skill for purpose-driven leaders who seek to understand, connect with, and support their team members.

Diversity and inclusion are critical components of any successful organization, and purpose-driven leaders understand this and actively work to create a culture that embraces both.

Firstly, purpose-driven leaders recognize the value of diversity in the workplace. Diversity brings different perspectives, experiences, and ideas to the table, which can lead to better problem-solving and innovation. Purpose- driven leaders actively seek out diverse candidates when hiring, and they create an environment where everyone feels welcome and valued.

In addition to hiring practices, purpose-driven leaders also ensure that their organization is inclusive. This means creating an environment where everyone feels comfortable sharing their ideas and opinions, regardless of their background or status within the organization. Purpose-driven leaders foster an inclusive culture by actively listening to their employees, encouraging open communication, and addressing any issues related to discrimination or bias.

Another important aspect of creating an inclusive culture is providing opportunities for growth and development. Purpose-driven leaders recognize that everyone has unique talents and skills, and they work to cultivate those strengths within their team. This means providing training and development opportunities that are accessible to everyone, regardless of their background or experience.

Establish clear diversity and inclusion goals: Purpose-driven leaders set clear goals for diversity and inclusion, and they hold themselves and their team accountable for achieving them. This may include setting targets for hiring diverse candidates, promoting diversity within leadership positions, or creating a more inclusive workplace culture.

Foster a sense of belonging: In addition to creating an inclusive culture, purpose-driven leaders also work to foster a sense of belonging among their employees. This means creating an environment where everyone feels valued, respected, and supported. Purpose-driven leaders may do this by hosting team-building activities, recognizing the achievements of team members, or providing opportunities for employees to give back to their community.

Encourage employee resource groups: Purpose-driven leaders recognize the importance of employee resource groups (ERGs) in creating a more inclusive workplace culture. ERGs provide a space for employees with shared interests or backgrounds to come together, share ideas, and support one another. Purpose-driven leaders encourage the formation of ERGs and support their activities.

Use data to measure progress: Purpose-driven leaders use data to measure their progress in creating a more diverse and inclusive workplace. They may track metrics such as employee demographics, turnover rates, or employee engagement scores to monitor progress and identify areas for improvement.

Lead by example: Finally, purpose-driven leaders lead by example when it comes to diversity and inclusion. They model the behavior they want to see in their organization by treating everyone with respect, listening to their employees, and actively working to create a culture of inclusion.

Provide training on diversity and inclusion: Purpose-driven leaders recognize that creating a diverse and inclusive workplace requires ongoing education and training. They provide opportunities for their employees to learn about diversity and inclusion and how it can benefit the organization. This may include training sessions, workshops, or online courses.

Address unconscious bias: Purpose-driven leaders understand that everyone has unconscious biases, and they work to address them within their organization. They may provide training on identifying and addressing unconscious bias or implement policies and processes that reduce the impact of bias on hiring and promotion decisions.

Celebrate diversity: Purpose-driven leaders celebrate the diversity within their organization by recognizing and honoring different cultures, traditions, and holidays. This can be done through events, social media posts, or other forms of communication.

Encourage mentorship and sponsorship: Purpose-driven leaders encourage mentorship and sponsorship programs that help diverse employees develop their skills and advance within the organization. They also create opportunities for diverse employees to share their knowledge and experience with others.

Collaborate with external organizations: Finally, purpose-driven leaders collaborate with external organizations that promote diversity and inclusion. This may include partnering with community groups, supporting diversity-focused nonprofits, or participating in industry-wide initiatives to increase diversity and inclusion. By working together, purpose-driven leaders can create a more inclusive workplace culture both within their organization and beyond.

Create a diverse leadership team: Purpose-driven leaders understand the importance of having diverse perspectives at the top of their organization. They actively seek out candidates from diverse backgrounds for leadership positions and work to create a leadership pipeline that reflects the diversity of their workforce.

Provide flexible work arrangements: Purpose-driven leaders recognize that their employees have different needs and responsibilities outside of work. They provide flexible work arrangements, such as remote work or flexible hours, to accommodate the needs of their diverse workforce.

Address microaggressions: Purpose-driven leaders address microaggressions, which are subtle forms of discrimination that can occur in the workplace. They provide training for their employees on how to recognize and address microaggressions and create a culture where everyone feels comfortable speaking up if they experience or witness them.

Create a safe reporting system: Purpose-driven leaders create a safe reporting system where employees can report instances of discrimination or bias without fear of retaliation. They take all reports seriously and investigate them thoroughly to ensure that everyone feels safe and supported in the workplace.

Measure impact: Finally, purpose-driven leaders measure the impact of their diversity and inclusion efforts on their organization. They regularly assess their progress towards their diversity and inclusion goals and make adjustments as necessary to ensure that they are making a positive impact on their workforce and the broader community.

Trust is indeed a crucial element of effective leadership. Purpose-driven leaders understand this and work to build trust with their followers. There are several ways in which purpose-driven leaders build trust:

Consistency: Purpose-driven leaders are consistent in their words and actions. They do what they say they will do, and they follow through on their commitments. This consistency builds trust with their followers, who can rely on them to be honest and dependable.

Integrity: Purpose-driven leaders have strong moral and ethical principles, and they act in accordance with those principles. They are transparent in their decision-making processes, and they communicate openly with their followers. This integrity builds trust with their followers, who know that their leader will always do what is right.

Empathy: Purpose-driven leaders show empathy towards their followers. They listen to their concerns, understand their perspectives, and act in their best interests. This empathy builds trust with their followers, who feel valued and respected by their leader.

Competence: Purpose-driven leaders are competent in their roles. They have the knowledge, skills, and experience necessary to lead their followers effectively. This competence builds trust with their followers, who have confidence in their leader's ability to make sound decisions and achieve their goals.

Vision: Purpose-driven leaders have a clear vision for the future, and they communicate that vision to their followers. They inspire their followers to work towards a common goal, and they provide direction and guidance along the way. This vision builds trust with their followers, who share their leader's sense of purpose and direction.

Authenticity: Purpose-driven leaders are authentic in their interactions with their followers. They are genuine and transparent, and they don't try to be someone they're not. This authenticity builds trust with their followers, who appreciate their leader's honesty and sincerity.

Accountability: Purpose-driven leaders hold themselves and their followers accountable for their actions and decisions. They take responsibility for their mistakes and learn from them, and they expect the same from their followers. This accountability builds trust with their followers, who know that their leader is fair and consistent in their expectations.

Inclusivity: Purpose-driven leaders value diversity and inclusivity, and they create a culture that respects and celebrates differences. They ensure that everyone has a voice and is treated with dignity and respect. This inclusivity builds trust with their followers, who feel valued and included in the organization's mission.

Collaboration: Purpose-driven leaders foster a culture of collaboration, where everyone works together towards a common goal. They encourage their followers to share ideas and opinions, and they facilitate open communication and feedback. This collaboration builds trust with their followers, who feel like they are part of a team that is working towards something meaningful.

Growth: Purpose-driven leaders prioritize growth and development for themselves and their followers. They invest in their own learning and seek out opportunities for personal and professional growth. They also provide their followers with opportunities for growth and development, and they support them in achieving their goals. This focus on growth builds trust with their followers, who feel like their leader is invested in their success and development.

Transparency: Purpose-driven leaders are transparent in their decision-making processes and communicate openly with their followers. They share information about the organization's goals, strategies, and challenges, and they involve their followers in important decisions. This transparency builds trust with their followers, who feel informed and included in the organization's direction.

Humility: Purpose-driven leaders are humble and recognize that they don't have all the answers. They are open to feedback and willing to admit when they are wrong. This humility builds trust with their followers, who appreciate their leader's willingness to listen and learn.

Compassion: Purpose-driven leaders show compassion towards their followers, especially during difficult times. They offer support and understanding, and they prioritize the well-being of their followers. This compassion builds trust with their followers, who feel that their leader cares about them as individuals.

Courage: Purpose-driven leaders have the courage to take risks and make difficult decisions when necessary. They are willing to challenge the status quo and push for change, even when it's unpopular. This courage builds trust with their followers, who respect their leader's willingness to take bold action.

Gratitude: Purpose-driven leaders express gratitude towards their followers and recognize their contributions. They celebrate successes and acknowledge the hard work and dedication of their followers. This gratitude builds trust with their followers, who feel appreciated and valued by their leader.

In summary, purpose-driven leaders build trust through transparency, humility, compassion, courage, and gratitude. By focusing on these qualities, purpose-driven leaders can create a culture of trust that inspires their followers to achieve great things and work towards a common purpose.

Collaboration is indeed crucial for purpose-driven leaders who want to achieve shared goals and create positive change. Building strong partnerships both within and outside of your organization is key to fostering collaboration. Here are some strategies that can help:

Build trust: Trust is the foundation of any successful collaboration. Establish clear communication channels, be transparent, and follow through on your commitments. Encourage open and honest feedback and actively listen to the views of others.

Define goals and roles: Clearly define the goals of the collaboration and the roles of each participant. Make sure everyone understands their responsibilities, and that they are aligned with the overall objectives.

Foster a collaborative culture: Create a culture that values collaboration and encourages teamwork. Reward collaboration, celebrate successes, and recognize individuals who contribute to the collaboration's success.

Use technology: Use technology to facilitate collaboration, whether it's through collaboration software, project management tools, or video conferencing. Ensure that everyone has access to the technology they need to participate fully in the collaboration.

Build relationships: Take the time to build relationships with your collaborators. Get to know them on a personal level, and understand their strengths and weaknesses. This will help to build trust and establish a strong foundation for collaboration.

Be adaptable: Collaboration requires flexibility and adaptability. Be prepared to adjust your plans and strategies as needed to accommodate changes in circumstances or new information.

Evaluate and adjust: Regularly evaluate the collaboration's progress and adjust your approach as needed. Solicit feedback from your collaborators and make changes based on their input.

Encourage diversity and inclusion: Embrace diversity and inclusion in your collaboration efforts. Seek out collaborators who bring different perspectives, experiences, and backgrounds to the table. Encourage open dialogue and respect for different opinions and viewpoints.

Establish clear communication: Clear communication is essential for successful collaboration. Establish guidelines for communication, such as regular check-ins, meeting agendas, and clear expectations for response times.

Set realistic expectations: Set realistic expectations for the collaboration's outcomes and timelines. Be honest about what is achievable, and don't overpromise. This will help to avoid disappointment and frustration down the line.

Build shared understanding: Take the time to build a shared understanding of the collaboration's objectives, priorities, and processes. This can involve creating a common language, sharing best practices, and establishing shared values.

Celebrate diversity of thought: Encourage collaborators to bring their unique perspectives to the table. Celebrate diversity of thought, and create a safe space for individuals to express their ideas and opinions.

Empower individuals: Empower individuals to take ownership of their roles and responsibilities within the collaboration. Provide them with the resources and support they need to succeed, and encourage them to take risks and innovate.

Share credit and recognition: Share credit and recognition for the collaboration's successes. Recognize the contributions of all collaborators, and acknowledge the role that each individual played in achieving the collaboration's goals.

Emphasize win-win outcomes: Focus on creating win-win outcomes that benefit all collaborators. This can involve finding common ground, identifying shared values, and working together to find creative solutions.

Prioritize relationship-building: Invest time and effort in building strong relationships with your collaborators. This can involve socializing outside of work, attending industry events together, or simply taking the time to get to know each other on a personal level.

Encourage experimentation and innovation: Encourage collaborators to experiment with new ideas and approaches, and to innovate to find more effective solutions. Create a culture that values learning from failure and encourages risk-taking.

Leverage strengths: Leverage the strengths of each collaborator to achieve the collaboration's goals. Identify each individual's unique talents and skills, and find ways to put them to use in the collaboration.

Foster a sense of belonging: Create a sense of belonging among collaborators by emphasizing the shared purpose and values that bring them together. Encourage a sense of community and shared ownership of the collaboration's outcomes.

Embrace feedback: Embrace feedback as a tool for continuous improvement. Encourage collaborators to provide feedback on the collaboration's processes and outcomes, and use that feedback to make adjustments and improve performance.

By implementing these strategies, you can foster a collaborative culture that supports your organization's mission and helps you achieve your shared goals. Remember that collaboration requires ongoing effort and attention, and that it is a process of continuous improvement. By continuously evaluating and adjusting your approach, you can build strong partnerships and achieve success together.

Leading with courage is indeed essential for purpose-driven leaders. Courage enables leaders to face challenges, take risks, and make difficult decisions that align with their purpose and values. Here are some key principles to keep in mind when leading with courage:

Know your purpose and values: A clear understanding of your purpose and values will help you make courageous decisions that align with your vision and mission. It's important to know what you stand for and what you're trying to achieve.

Take calculated risks: Courage doesn't mean being reckless. It means taking calculated risks based on data, analysis, and intuition. Assess the potential risks and rewards of each decision, and make a well-informed choice.

Be prepared to fail: Courageous leaders understand that failure is a possibility. They don't let the fear of failure hold them back from taking action. Instead, they learn from their mistakes and use them as opportunities to grow and improve.

Communicate effectively: Courageous leaders communicate their vision and decisions clearly and effectively. They listen to feedback and concerns from their team members and stakeholders, and address them in a transparent and respectful manner.

Lead by example: Courageous leaders lead by example. They demonstrate the values and behaviors they expect from their team members, and they don't shy away from difficult conversations or actions.

Embrace discomfort: Courageous leaders are willing to step outside of their comfort zones and embrace discomfort. They recognize that growth and progress often require taking risks and facing uncertainty.

Seek diverse perspectives: Courageous leaders seek out diverse perspectives and opinions, even if they challenge their own views.

They recognize that a diversity of perspectives can help them make more informed and effective decisions.

Stand up for what's right: Courageous leaders are willing to stand up for what's right, even in the face of opposition or adversity. They prioritize ethics and integrity, and hold themselves and their team members accountable for their actions.

Build resilience: Leading with courage can be challenging and exhausting. Building resilience through self-care, support networks, and stress management techniques can help leaders stay strong and focused in the face of challenges.

Celebrate successes: Finally, courageous leaders celebrate their successes, both big and small. They recognize the hard work and risks taken by themselves and their team members, and take time to acknowledge and appreciate their accomplishments.

Stay true to your values: Courageous leaders are guided by their values and principles, even when it's difficult or unpopular. They don't compromise their values for short-term gains or to please others.

Foster a culture of courage: Courageous leaders foster a culture of courage by encouraging and empowering their team members to take risks, share their ideas, and speak up. They create an environment where people feel safe to take calculated risks and learn from their mistakes.

Learn from failure: Courageous leaders view failure as an opportunity to learn and grow. They don't dwell on mistakes or blame others, but instead, they analyze what went wrong, identify lessons learned, and use them to improve their future decisions.

Build trust: Courageous leaders build trust with their team members and stakeholders through open communication, transparency, and consistency. They keep their promises and commitments, admit their mistakes, and act with integrity.

Continuously learn and adapt: Courageous leaders are lifelong learners who continuously seek new knowledge, skills, and experiences. They are adaptable and agile, able to pivot and adjust their strategies as needed to achieve their goals.

Be authentic: Courageous leaders are authentic and genuine in their interactions with others. They don't put on a facade or try to be someone they're not. They are true to themselves and their values, and that authenticity inspires others to follow their lead.

Encourage creativity and innovation: Courageous leaders encourage creativity and innovation in their team members. They create a culture where new ideas are welcomed, and people are encouraged to think outside the box.

Take a long-term perspective: Courageous leaders take a long-term perspective and think about the impact of their decisions on future generations. They are willing to make short-term sacrifices for long-term gains and sustainability.

Develop emotional intelligence: Courageous leaders develop emotional intelligence, which enables them to understand and manage their own emotions and those of others. Emotional intelligence helps them navigate difficult conversations and situations with empathy and compassion.

Surround yourself with support: Finally, courageous leaders surround themselves with support, whether it's through mentors, coaches, peers, or family and friends. They seek out people who can provide guidance, feedback, and encouragement, and who can help them stay focused and resilient in the face of challenges.

By following these tips, purpose-driven leaders can continue to lead with courage and make a positive impact on the world. Courageous leadership is a journey, and it requires ongoing learning, self-reflection, and growth. But with perseverance and a commitment to their purpose and values, leaders can inspire others and achieve their goals.

Leading through change requires a combination of strategic planning, effective communication, and a willingness to adapt to new circumstances. Here are some key steps that purpose-driven leaders can take to navigate change effectively:

Establish a clear vision and communicate it effectively: During times of change, it's important to have a clear vision of where the organization is headed and to communicate that vision to all stakeholders. This helps to provide a sense of direction and purpose, and can help to align everyone around a common goal.

Engage and involve stakeholders: Change can be unsettling for people, so it's important to involve stakeholders in the process and keep them informed about what's happening. This can help to build trust and buy-in, and can also provide valuable input and feedback.

Develop a change management plan: A comprehensive change management plan can help to ensure that the organization is prepared for the changes ahead. This plan should include a timeline, milestones, and metrics for measuring progress, as well as strategies for mitigating risks and addressing any challenges that arise.

Foster a culture of resilience and adaptability: Change can be difficult, but it's important to foster a culture of resilience and adaptability within the organization. This means encouraging innovation, experimentation, and a willingness to take calculated risks. It also means providing support and resources to help people navigate change and develop new skills.

Monitor and adjust as needed: Finally, it's important to monitor progress and adjust the change management plan as needed. This means being flexible and responsive to new information, and being willing to pivot if necessary.

Build a strong team: During times of change, it's important to have a strong team in place that can help to drive the organization forward. This means hiring and developing people who are resilient, adaptable, and committed to the organization's purpose and values.

Embrace technology: Technology can be a powerful tool for driving change and innovation, so purpose-driven leaders should be open to adopting new technologies that can help to streamline processes, improve communication, and drive growth.

Celebrate success: Change can be difficult, but it's important to celebrate successes along the way. This helps to build momentum and maintain a positive attitude, and can also provide a sense of accomplishment and satisfaction for everyone involved.

Learn from failures: Change is not always smooth sailing, and purpose-driven leaders should be prepared to learn from failures and setbacks along the way. This means being open to feedback, analyzing what went wrong, and making adjustments as needed.

Stay true to your purpose: Finally, it's important to stay true to the organization's purpose and values, even during times of change. This means making decisions that align with the organization's mission and goals, and being transparent and honest with stakeholders about the reasons behind any changes.

Communicate with empathy: Change can be a challenging and emotional experience for people, so it's important for purpose-driven leaders to communicate with empathy. This means acknowledging people's concerns and fears, and providing support and reassurance as needed.

Create a sense of urgency: Change can be difficult to achieve if people don't see a compelling reason for it. Purpose- driven leaders should create a sense of urgency around the changes they want to make, highlighting the benefits and opportunities that come with it.

Be transparent: During times of change, it's important to be transparent with stakeholders about what's happening and why. This means being honest about any challenges or risks, as well as the steps being taken to address them.

Invest in employee development: Change often requires new skills and knowledge, so purpose-driven leaders should invest in employee development to ensure that people have the tools they need to succeed.

Build partnerships: Change can be easier to achieve when multiple stakeholders are involved. Purpose-driven leaders should look for opportunities to build partnerships and collaborations with other organizations, stakeholders, and communities to drive change and achieve shared goals.

Encourage open communication: During times of change, it's important to encourage open communication and feedback from stakeholders. This means creating channels for people to ask questions, share concerns, and provide input, and actively listening to their feedback.

Foster a culture of continuous improvement: Change is often an ongoing process, so purpose-driven leaders should foster a culture of continuous improvement within the organization. This means encouraging people to identify areas for improvement, experiment with new ideas, and learn from their experiences.

Measure and track progress: To ensure that the organization is making progress towards its goals, purpose-driven leaders should establish metrics and track progress over time. This helps to ensure accountability and transparency, and can also provide valuable insights into what's working and what's not.

Anticipate and plan for future changes: Change is inevitable, so purpose-driven leaders should anticipate and plan for future changes as much as possible. This means staying informed about trends and developments in the industry and the broader environment, and proactively seeking out opportunities for innovation and growth.

Lead by example: Finally, purpose-driven leaders should lead by example during times of change. This means embodying the organization's purpose and values, staying positive and optimistic, and modeling the behaviors and attitudes that are needed to drive change and achieve success.

By employing these strategies, purpose-driven leaders can successfully navigate change while maintaining a sense of purpose and direction for their organization, and ensuring that everyone involved is engaged, informed, and supported.

Balancing short-term and long-term goals is a critical skill for purpose-driven leaders. Short-term goals are essential for keeping a business running smoothly and addressing immediate challenges, while long-term goals help to ensure lasting success and continued growth. However, it can be challenging to balance these two priorities, as short-term goals often demand immediate attention and can overshadow longer-term objectives.

To achieve sustainable success, purpose-driven leaders must find a way to balance these competing priorities. Here are some strategies to help you achieve this:

Set clear goals: Clearly define your short-term and long-term goals, and make sure they align with your overall purpose and vision. This will help you prioritize your efforts and stay focused on what matters most.

Prioritize: When faced with competing priorities, prioritize tasks that align with your long-term goals. This will help you build momentum and make progress toward achieving your purpose and vision.

Be flexible: Be prepared to adjust your plans as needed. Sometimes short-term goals may need to take precedence over longer-term objectives, but always keep your purpose and vision in mind.

Communicate: Communicate your goals and priorities to your team, stakeholders, and customers. This will help build trust and support for your purpose-driven approach.

Measure progress: Regularly measure progress toward both short-term and long-term goals. This will help you stay on track and make adjustments as needed.

Delegate: Delegate tasks that are not directly related to your purpose and vision, so that you can focus on the big picture. This will help you free up time and energy to work on longer-term goals.

Invest in people: Invest in your team and stakeholders, as they are instrumental in helping you achieve your purpose and vision. Support their growth and development, and foster a culture of collaboration and innovation.

Stay agile: Stay agile and adaptable in the face of changing circumstances. This will help you stay relevant and responsive to emerging trends and challenges.

Embrace innovation: Embrace innovation and experimentation, as this can lead to breakthroughs that support your purpose and vision. Encourage your team to think creatively and take calculated risks.

Stay true to your values: Finally, stay true to your values and principles, even when faced with short-term pressures or difficult decisions. This will help you maintain your integrity and build a strong foundation for lasting success.

Focus on impact: Rather than focusing solely on outputs and immediate results, focus on the long-term impact of your work. This will help you prioritize efforts that will have the greatest positive impact on your stakeholders and society as a whole.

Foster a learning culture: Encourage a culture of learning and continuous improvement, so that you and your team can adapt to changing circumstances and stay ahead of the curve.

Build strategic partnerships: Build strategic partnerships with other organizations and stakeholders who share your purpose and vision. This will help you leverage collective strengths and resources to achieve common goals.

Communicate progress: Communicate progress toward your short-term and long-term goals regularly to your team, stakeholders, and customers. This will help build transparency and trust, and keep everyone aligned with your purpose and vision.

Be patient: Balancing short-term and long-term goals takes time and patience. Don't get discouraged if progress is slow or if you encounter obstacles along the way. Stay committed to your purpose and vision, and keep moving forward.

Emphasize collaboration: Encourage collaboration and cross-functional teamwork to help balance short-term and long-term goals. This will help ensure that all stakeholders are aligned and working together toward a common purpose.

Use data and analytics: Use data and analytics to inform your decision-making and help balance short-term and long-term goals. This will help you make more informed decisions and stay on track.

Empower your team: Empower your team to take ownership of short-term and long-term goals, and give them the resources and support they need to succeed. This will help build a sense of collective purpose and foster a culture of accountability.

Stay grounded in your purpose: Always stay grounded in your purpose and values, and use them as a guidepost when making decisions. This will help ensure that your actions are aligned with your purpose and vision.

Celebrate successes: Finally, celebrate successes along the way, both short-term and long-term. This will help build momentum and motivation, and reinforce the importance of your purpose-driven approach.

In summary, balancing short-term and long-term goals as a purpose-driven leader requires a combination of strategies, including collaboration, data and analytics, empowering your team, staying grounded in your purpose, and celebrating successes. With these strategies in place, you can make strategic decisions that support your purpose and vision, and achieve lasting impact for your organization and stakeholders.

Leading with authenticity means being true to yourself and your values, while also being genuine and transparent in your interactions with others. It involves being honest, vulnerable, and courageous in your leadership style, and being willing to share your personal experiences and emotions with those around you.

To lead with authenticity, it's important to first identify your purpose and values. Your purpose is the reason that you exist, and your values are the guiding principles that you live by. Once you have a clear understanding of these, you can begin to align your actions and decisions with them, and communicate them to others in a way that is clear and consistent.

Another key aspect of leading with authenticity is building trust with your team. Trust is the foundation of any strong relationship, and it is crucial for effective leadership. To build trust, it's important to be transparent and honest in your communications, and to follow through on your commitments. It's also important to show empathy and understanding towards your team members, and to create a culture of psychological safety where they feel comfortable sharing their thoughts and ideas.

Leading with authenticity also means being willing to learn and grow. No one is perfect, and it's important to acknowledge your mistakes and weaknesses, and to work on improving yourself as a leader. This involves seeking feedback from others, being open to new ideas and perspectives, and continuously developing your skills and knowledge.

Be yourself: Authentic leaders don't try to be someone they're not. They embrace their unique strengths, weaknesses, and quirks, and allow their personality to shine through in their leadership style.

Listen actively: Authentic leaders are good listeners. They take the time to understand their team members' perspectives, and they show empathy and understanding towards their needs and concerns.

Communicate clearly: Authentic leaders are transparent and clear in their communications. They don't hide behind jargon or corporate speak, and they are willing to have difficult conversations when necessary.

Live your values: Authentic leaders lead by example. They embody their values in their daily actions and decisions, and they hold themselves accountable to the same standards they expect of others.

Embrace vulnerability: Authentic leaders are not afraid to be vulnerable. They are willing to share their personal experiences and emotions with others, and they see vulnerability as a strength, not a weakness.

Lead with purpose: Authentic leaders have a clear sense of purpose that drives their actions and decisions. They are committed to making a positive impact in the world, and they inspire others to do the same.

Build strong relationships: Authentic leaders prioritize building strong relationships with their team members and stakeholders. They take the time to get to know people on a personal level, and they create a culture of trust and respect.

Be adaptable: Authentic leaders are able to adapt their leadership style to different situations and individuals. They recognize that each person is unique, and they adjust their approach accordingly.

Focus on the big picture: Authentic leaders have a clear vision of where they want to go, and they focus on the big picture. They don't get bogged down in the details, but they keep their eye on the ultimate goal.

Encourage creativity and innovation: Authentic leaders encourage creativity and innovation in their team members. They create a safe space where people feel free to share their ideas and take risks.

Empower your team: Authentic leaders empower their team members to take ownership of their work and make decisions. They provide guidance and support, but they also give people the freedom to explore their own ideas and solutions.

Take responsibility: Authentic leaders take responsibility for their actions and decisions. They don't blame others when things go wrong, but they take ownership of the situation and work to find a solution.

Seek out diverse perspectives: Authentic leaders seek out diverse perspectives and opinions from people with different backgrounds and experiences. They recognize the value of different viewpoints and use them to make more informed decisions.

Leading with authenticity is about being genuine, transparent, and true to yourself and your values. By following these tips, you can create a culture of trust and respect, and inspire your team to achieve great things.

Be present: Authentic leaders are fully present in the moment, whether they are interacting with team members, making decisions, or pursuing their goals. They are not distracted by other things, and they give their full attention to the task at hand.

Be accountable: Authentic leaders hold themselves and their team members accountable for their actions and decisions. They are not afraid to take responsibility for mistakes and failures, and they work to learn from them and improve.

Practice active listening: Authentic leaders practice active listening, which means they listen with the intention of understanding, not just responding. They seek to understand the other person's perspective and emotions before offering their own thoughts or opinions.

Build a culture of feedback: Authentic leaders create a culture of feedback where team members feel comfortable sharing their thoughts and opinions. They provide constructive feedback to help people grow and improve, and they also solicit feedback from others to improve their own leadership.

Be inclusive: Authentic leaders are inclusive and value diversity. They recognize that everyone has something to contribute, regardless of their background or experiences, and they create a welcoming environment where everyone feels valued and respected.

Lead by example: Authentic leaders lead by example and set the tone for their team. They model the behavior they want to see in their team members, and they demonstrate their commitment to their values and purpose through their actions.

Leading with authenticity is about being true to yourself and your values, while also creating a culture of trust, respect, and inclusivity. By following these tips, you can inspire your team to achieve great things and make a positive impact in the world.

Mentoring and developing others is an essential aspect of leadership. Purpose-driven leaders understand that investing in the development of their team is crucial to achieving sustainable success. By supporting the growth and development of their team members, leaders can create a culture of continuous learning that benefits everyone involved.

There are several key strategies that purpose-driven leaders can use to mentor and develop others:

Set clear expectations: Leaders should establish clear expectations for their team members, including performance goals, development objectives, and timelines for achieving these goals. Clear expectations provide team members with a roadmap for success and help them stay motivated and focused.

Provide feedback: Regular feedback is critical to helping team members grow and develop. Purpose-driven leaders should provide both positive and constructive feedback to their team members on a regular basis. This feedback should be specific, actionable, and focused on helping team members improve their skills and performance.

Encourage learning: Leaders should encourage their team members to pursue learning opportunities, whether through formal training programs, mentoring relationships, or self-directed learning. Leaders can create a culture of continuous learning by modeling a commitment to learning themselves and providing resources and support to help their team members grow and develop.

Build relationships: Purpose-driven leaders should invest time and energy in building strong relationships with their team members. By getting to know team members on a personal level, leaders can better understand their strengths, weaknesses, and career aspirations. This insight can inform development plans and help leaders provide tailored support to each team member.

Lead by example: Purpose-driven leaders should model the behavior they want to see in their team members. This means demonstrating a commitment to learning, seeking out feedback, and continuously improving their own skills and performance.

Provide opportunities for growth: Leaders should provide opportunities for team members to take on new challenges and responsibilities. This can include stretch assignments, cross-functional projects, or leadership roles within the team. These opportunities allow team members to develop new skills and gain valuable experience

Celebrate successes: Purpose-driven leaders should recognize and celebrate the successes of their team members. This not only boosts team morale but also reinforces the importance of learning and development. Celebrating successes can also help team members feel valued and motivated to continue their growth and development.

Foster a growth mindset: Leaders should foster a growth mindset within their team by encouraging team members to embrace challenges, learn from failures, and persist in the face of obstacles. This mindset can help team members stay motivated and focused on their development goals.

Provide resources and support: Leaders should provide their team members with the resources and support they need to succeed. This can include access to training programs, coaching, mentorship, and other development resources.

Leaders should also be available to provide guidance and support as needed.

Create a safe and supportive environment: Purpose-driven leaders should create a safe and supportive environment where team members feel comfortable taking risks and trying new things. This can involve creating an open-door policy, encouraging feedback, and creating a culture of psychological safety where team members feel comfortable sharing their thoughts and ideas.

Encourage collaboration: Purpose-driven leaders should encourage their team members to collaborate and share knowledge with one another. This can involve creating opportunities for team members to work together on projects, facilitating knowledge-sharing sessions, or encouraging peer mentoring relationships.

Provide opportunities for feedback: Leaders should create opportunities for team members to provide feedback on their own development progress as well as on the development of their peers. This can involve regular check-ins, feedback surveys, or other mechanisms for collecting feedback.

Tailor development plans: Leaders should develop individualized development plans for each team member based on their unique strengths, weaknesses, and career aspirations. These plans should be regularly reviewed and updated to ensure that they remain relevant and aligned with the organization's goals.

Foster diversity and inclusion: Purpose-driven leaders should foster a diverse and inclusive environment where team members from different backgrounds and perspectives feel welcome and valued. This can involve creating policies and practices that promote diversity and inclusion, providing training to address unconscious bias and other forms of discrimination, and creating opportunities for team members to learn from one another.

Lead with empathy: Purpose-driven leaders should lead with empathy and compassion, taking the time to understand the needs and concerns of their team members. This can involve active listening, recognizing and addressing sources of stress and burnout, and providing emotional support when needed.

Encourage reflection: Leaders should encourage their team members to take time for reflection and self-assessment. This can involve regularly checking in with team members to discuss their progress toward their development goals, encouraging them to reflect on their own strengths and weaknesses, and providing tools and resources to support self-assessment.

Provide stretch assignments: Leaders should provide team members with stretch assignments that challenge them to develop new skills and take on new responsibilities. Stretch assignments can help team members build confidence, develop new skills, and gain valuable experience.

Encourage experimentation: Leaders should encourage team members to experiment and try new things, even if they are not sure of the outcome. This can involve creating a safe space for team members to take risks, providing resources and support to help them succeed, and celebrating their successes.

Foster a culture of innovation: Purpose-driven leaders should foster a culture of innovation within their team by encouraging team members to think creatively and come up with new ideas. This can involve providing resources and support for innovation, recognizing and rewarding innovative thinking, and creating opportunities for team members to collaborate on new ideas.

Lead with integrity: Purpose-driven leaders should lead with integrity and model the values and behaviors they want to see in their team members. This can involve being transparent and honest in their communications, treating team members with respect and fairness, and holding themselves accountable for their own development and growth.

By following these strategies, purpose-driven leaders can create a culture of continuous learning and development that supports the growth and success of their team members. This not only benefits individual team members but also contributes to the long-term success of the organization as a whole.

Sustaining purpose-driven leadership requires ongoing effort and commitment from leaders and their organizations. Here are some key strategies to help leaders sustain purpose-driven leadership:

Continuously communicate the purpose: Purpose-driven leadership is all about aligning the organization's goals and actions with a higher purpose. Therefore, it is essential to continuously communicate the purpose to all stakeholders, including employees, customers, shareholders, and the wider community. This communication should be done through multiple channels and platforms, such as town hall meetings, company newsletters, social media, and other forms of internal and external communication.

Embed the purpose in the culture: Purpose-driven leadership should be embedded in the culture of the organization, and leaders should consistently model behaviors aligned with the purpose. This involves creating a culture where employees feel valued, empowered, and motivated to contribute to the purpose. It also means aligning the organization's policies, processes, and systems with the purpose, so that everyone in the organization is working towards the same goal.

Measure and track progress: Purpose-driven leadership requires ongoing measurement and tracking of progress towards the purpose. This involves setting goals and metrics that align with the purpose and regularly monitoring and reporting on progress. Leaders should use data and analytics to identify areas of improvement and adjust strategies accordingly.

Foster collaboration and partnerships: Purpose-driven leadership requires collaboration and partnerships with stakeholders, such as customers, suppliers, NGOs, and other organizations. Collaborating with like-minded organizations can help to amplify the impact of purpose-driven initiatives and foster innovation.

Continuously learn and adapt: Purpose-driven leadership

requires a mindset of continuous learning and adaptation. Leaders should encourage experimentation and embrace failure as an opportunity to learn and improve. They should also stay up-to-date with the latest trends and best practices in purpose-driven leadership and be willing to adapt their strategies accordingly.

Invest in employee development: Purpose-driven leadership requires a highly engaged and motivated workforce. Therefore, it is essential to invest in employee development, including training, coaching, and mentoring. This investment should focus on developing employees' skills, knowledge, and mindset to align with the purpose and support the organization's goals.

Celebrate successes and recognize contributions: Purpose-driven leadership requires recognition and celebration of successes and contributions towards the purpose. Leaders should regularly acknowledge and celebrate achievements, both big and small, and recognize individuals and teams who have made significant contributions towards the purpose. This recognition helps to reinforce the importance of the purpose and motivate employees to continue their efforts.

Engage in continuous stakeholder dialogue: Purpose-driven leadership requires ongoing engagement with stakeholders to understand their needs, concerns, and expectations. Leaders should engage in continuous dialogue with stakeholders, including customers, employees, shareholders, and the wider community. This dialogue should be used to gather feedback, insights, and ideas to inform the organization's purpose-driven initiatives and strategies.

Build resilience and agility: Purpose-driven leadership requires resilience and agility to navigate challenges and uncertainties. Leaders should build resilience and agility by fostering a culture of innovation, experimentation, and risk-taking. They should also invest in technologies and processes that enable the organization to respond quickly and effectively to changing circumstances.

Embed purpose-driven leadership in the governance structure: Purpose-driven leadership should be embedded in the governance structure of the organization. This involves aligning the organization's governance structure with the purpose and ensuring that the purpose is reflected in the board's agenda, decision-making processes, and performance evaluation criteria.

Foster a culture of diversity, equity, and inclusion: Purpose-driven leadership requires a culture of diversity, equity, and inclusion (DEI) to ensure that all stakeholders are represented and valued. Leaders should foster a culture of DEI by promoting diversity in hiring, creating equal opportunities for all employees, and addressing any biases or discrimination that may exist within the organization. This will help to ensure that the organization's purpose-driven initiatives are inclusive and equitable.

Collaborate with external stakeholders: Purpose-driven leadership requires collaboration with external stakeholders, including NGOs, government agencies, and other organizations. Leaders should collaborate with these stakeholders to leverage their expertise, resources, and networks to advance the organization's purpose-driven initiatives. This collaboration can help to amplify the impact of purpose-driven initiatives and build partnerships that support long- term sustainability.

Align purpose-driven initiatives with the UN Sustainable Development Goals (SDGs): Purpose-driven leadership should align with the UN SDGs to ensure that the organization's purpose-driven initiatives address global challenges and contribute to sustainable development. Leaders should identify which SDGs are most relevant to their organization's purpose and align their initiatives with those goals. This alignment will help to ensure that the organization's purpose-driven initiatives are impactful and contribute to the global sustainable development agenda.

Continuously innovate and improve: Purpose-driven

leadership requires continuous innovation and improvement to stay relevant and effective. Leaders should encourage innovation and experimentation to identify new ways to advance the organization's purpose-driven initiatives. They should also continuously evaluate and improve their purpose-driven initiatives to ensure that they are achieving their intended outcomes.

Lead by example: Purpose-driven leadership requires leaders to lead by example and model behaviors aligned with the organization's purpose. Leaders should embody the values and principles of the purpose and demonstrate their commitment to the purpose through their actions and decisions. This will help to build trust and credibility with stakeholders and inspire others to follow their lead.

In conclusion, leading with purpose is essential for creating positive change and achieving long-term success in today's complex and rapidly changing world. Purpose-driven leadership involves aligning an organization's goals and actions with a higher purpose that goes beyond financial performance and focuses on creating value for all stakeholders, including employees, customers, shareholders, and the wider community.

By following these strategies, leaders can sustain purpose-driven leadership and create positive change that benefits all stakeholders. Purpose-driven leadership is not only beneficial for the organization but also for society as a whole, as it contributes to the greater good and helps to address some of the world's most pressing challenges. Therefore, leading with purpose is not only the right thing to do but also the smart thing to do.

AUTHOR'S NOTE

I write to you today as a leadership mentor, dedicated to empowering individuals like you who are determined to transform their lives. Within each and every one of us lies an incredible power—the power of mindset and the power of purpose. These two forces, when harnessed and nurtured, have the potential to shape our destinies and bring about remarkable achievements.

First and foremost, let us explore the power of mindset. Our minds are extraordinary tools that can either limit or liberate us. It is within our thoughts that the seeds of success or failure are sown. Remember, it is not the circumstances that define us, but rather the way we choose to perceive and respond to those circumstances. By cultivating a positive and resilient mindset, we can overcome obstacles, transcend limitations, and unleash our true potential.

Believe in the immense power within you. Embrace a mindset of possibility, where challenges become opportunities for growth and setbacks serve as stepping stones to success. Replace self- doubt with self-belief, and fear with unwavering courage. Remember, you have the capacity to shape your own reality through the power of your thoughts.

Now, let us explore the power of purpose. Purpose serves as the compass that guides us on our journey of personal growth and transformation. It is the driving force behind our actions, the fuel that propels us forward even in the face of adversity. When we align ourselves with a clear and meaningful purpose, we tap into a wellspring of motivation, focus, and resilience.

Discover your purpose by reflecting on your passions, values, and the impact you wish to make in the world. Embrace it wholeheartedly and infuse it into every aspect of your life. Let your purpose be the beacon that lights your path, even when the road ahead seems uncertain. With purpose as your guiding star, you will find the strength and determination to overcome any obstacle and achieve greatness.

Remember, your mindset and purpose are interconnected. A strong and positive mindset fuels your purpose, while a clear sense of purpose nurtures your mindset. Together, they form an unstoppable force that propels you towards your dreams and aspirations.

In your pursuit of dynamic change, be patient and persistent. Rome wasn't built in a day, and true transformation takes time. Embrace the journey, for it is through the challenges and setbacks that we grow and evolve. Surround yourself with like-minded individuals who uplift and inspire you, and seek out mentors who can guide you along the way.

You are capable of rewriting your story, of transcending your limitations, and of achieving greatness. Believe in yourself, harness the power of your mindset, and align yourself with a purpose that ignites your soul. Embrace the journey with unwavering determination, and let the world bear witness to the incredible transformation you are capable of.

With utmost faith in your potential,

Digvijay Mourya

ABOUT THE AUTHOR

Digvijay Mourya is a highly accomplished chemical engineer with an MBA and over 35 years of work experience, including 20 years in leadership positions. He has made significant contributions to the field of chemical engineering and has demonstrated exceptional leadership skills throughout his career.

Currently, Digvijay Mourya serves as the CEO of an industrial house, where he oversees all operations and strategic initiatives. Under his leadership, the company has achieved significant growth and success, expanding its reach to new markets and driving innovation in the industry.

Prior to his current role, Digvijay Mourya held various leadership positions in several renowned organizations, where he was responsible for developing and executing business strategies, managing teams, and driving growth.

Beyond his professional achievements, Digvijay Mourya is known for his integrity, dedication, and passion for mentoring young professionals. He is committed to giving back to his community and has been actively involved in several social and environmental initiatives.

Overall, Digvijay Mourya's extensive work experience, exceptional leadership skills, and commitment to excellence make him a highly respected and sought-after professional in the industry.

Also by Digvijay Mourya

Leading and Selling

INKFEATHERS
PUBLISHING
www.inkfeathers.com

www.ingramcontent.com/pod-product-compliance
Lightning Source LLC
LaVergne TN
LVHW091212150826
845672LV00005B/1318